COLLEGE 101

College 101: A Girl's Guide to Freshman Year is a comprehensive and authentic guide for girls to everything college from girls who have been through it!

Combining honest, humorous, and relatable first-person perspectives with expert advice, this dynamic guide shows girls what to really expect from their first year of college, including pro tips and common pitfalls to avoid. From managing academics and navigating new social situations, to avoiding debt and getting enough sleep, this book honestly answers all your questions about university life, including those you didn't even know you had!

Full of valuable information and must-know secrets about freshman year, *College 101* is a must-read for girls who want not only to survive but also actually enjoy their first college experience.

Julie Zeilinger is a writer, editor, and Barnard College alumna. She is the founder of the WMC FBomb, a blog for young feminists affiliated with the Women's Media Center, and the author of *A Little F'd Up: Why Feminism Is Not a Dirty Word* (2012).

Anna Koppelman is a New York-based writer. At 15, she began publishing her writing on the excitement, heartbreak, and wonder of growing up in national outlets like MTV, the *Huffington Post*, and *Entertainment Weekly*.

Top Advice From Girls Who Have Been Through It!

Third Edition

COLLEGE 101

A Girl's Guide to Freshman Year

Julie Zeilinger
with Anna Koppelman

Routledge
Taylor & Francis Group

NEW YORK AND LONDON

Designed cover image: Getty

First published 2024
by Routledge
605 Third Avenue, New York, NY 10158

and by Routledge
4 Park Square, Milton Park, Abingdon, Oxon, OX14 4RN

Routledge is an imprint of the Taylor & Francis Group, an informa business

© 2024 Julie Zeilinger

Library of Congress Cataloging-in-Publication Data
Names: Zeilinger, Julie, 1993– author.
Title: College 101 : a girl's guide to freshman year /
Julie Zeilinger with Anna Koppelman.
Description: Third edition. | New York, NY : Routledge, 2024. |
Includes bibliographical references and index. |
Identifiers: LCCN 2023055688 (print) | LCCN 2023055689 (ebook) |
ISBN 9781032525235 (paperback) | ISBN 9781003408932 (ebook)
Subjects: LCSH: College student orientation–United States. |
Women college students–United States–Life skills guides. |
College freshmen–United States–Life skills guides.
Classification: LCC LB2343.32 .Z45 2024 (print) |
LCC LB2343.32 (ebook) | DDC 378.1/98–dc23/eng/20231207
LC record available at https://lccn.loc.gov/2023055688
LC ebook record available at https://lccn.loc.gov/2023055689

ISBN: 978-1-032-52523-5 (pbk)
ISBN: 978-1-003-40893-2 (ebk)

DOI: 10.4324/9781003408932

Typeset in Minion
by Newgen Publishing UK

CONTENTS

CHAPTER 1

WHAT COLLEGE IS REALLY LIKE

Congratulations—you've made it to the first page of this book, which means you're soon going to college (or presumably at least have some kind of vague interest in college). As two women who have successfully made it through our college experiences, we're here to help.

Julie Zeilinger wrote the first edition of this book soon after she completed her freshman year of college. She expected college to be the best four years of her life and was surprised to find that wasn't quite the case (more on that soon). She decided to write the guide she could've used beforehand to navigate the gap between her expectations for college and the reality of the experience.

She wrote that guide, however, way back in 2014, and a decade later, many things about the college experience have changed. So she called up her friend Anna Koppelman, who graduated college much more recently, to help fill in the gaps. Anna is a part of the class of 2022, but she's still aware of how much has already changed since then. When she got into school in 2018, there was still a

DOI: 10.4324/9781003408932-1

class Facebook page. Sure, it felt like a kind of cool vintage relic of college orientation years prior, but there was one! Now, class Facebook pages have become class Instagrams, and it's getting harder for Anna to say she "just graduated college." While Anna adored college, there are so many things she wishes she could go back and tell her freshman-year self—and she's going to share them here.

A lot has changed over the past decade, but we agree that one thing has stayed the same: The wildly popular myth that college will be the best four years of your life is just that—a myth. We really don't think college will be the Best Experience of Your Life. In fact, we sincerely hope it's not.

That being said, we understand the impulse to glorify the undergraduate experience. Even if the very act of going to college is a financial burden (and we will discuss that in greater depth—we have some capital F Feelings about the student loan situation), a lot of people make the case that it's basically the ultimate sweet spot: You have enough freedom to make your own decisions and to have a ton of fun whenever you want, but not so much freedom that you have to worry about adult responsibilities like paying loads of taxes. Your job is to learn, to have fun, and to *discover yourself* (in terms of your mind *and* body).

Here's the thing, though: *College isn't really like that.*

Well, okay, it is like that in a superficial way. Most myths about college are true on some level, and college certainly isn't like a Dickensian orphanage—you do discover new things about yourself, have plenty of fun, and even learn a thing or two. But the depiction of college as a manic experience of free love and nonstop partying only scrapes the surface of what college is really like. Like most things in life, college is full of highs *and* lows and experiences that aren't necessarily good or bad. And yet, we're all pretty dedicated to maintaining a culture of silence about our struggles, about bolstering the myth that college is a giant, equalizing party when the freshman year experience can also be isolating, difficult, and even downright scary.

The thing is, if we were all more transparent about our struggles as freshmen (and beyond), we would find that most of us feel the same way—which would probably make everybody feel *a lot* better. Openness and honesty don't erase difficult experiences, but they can make them a little easier to navigate to one's advantage. We need to be honest about college and present it as a nuanced experience.

Enter this book. Drawing from our own experiences, the experiences of college-aged women who just went through this process, and various experts, we hope to debunk most of these myths, big and small, so that you don't have to reinvent the wheel and instead can embrace and learn from the experiences of those who have already been there. Basically, we're going to give you all the advice, tips, and facts we wish we had when—bright-eyed and bushy-tailed—we first stepped foot on our campuses.

We'll tell you the truth about everything from what to expect in the classroom (how to get ahead and, yes, when to take a step back) and (mostly) what to expect outside of it. We'll discuss roommates, relationships, hooking up, and sex (and none of that vague, wishy-washy advice—the *real* stuff), as well as more serious, yet very real and pervasive issues like sexual health and violence. We'll even talk about debt, but not in an economic, droning way: in the straightforward need-to-know, this-is-how-we-can-avoid-getting-screwed-over way. And those are just the highlights.

Of course, most of the advice in this book is applicable to students of all genders. But we do think people who identify as women have unique emotional, psychological, and academic experiences that *are* different from others' experiences, so we'll focus on those in particular throughout this book.

But before we get into the details, let's look at the big picture and debunk the biggest overarching myths of all.

MYTH: Adapting to college is not a big deal—after orientation, you're totally set, and if you're not having the most fun ever all the time, then you're doing it wrong.

TRUTH: Freshman year can be a real bitch.

Like most other newbies, Julie went off to college her freshman year way back in 2011 under the impression that she was headed toward the greatest experience of her life. Hastily constructed college movies full of crappy dialogue and 30-year-old actors with perfect faces and bodies cast as 18-year-old freshmen had completely swayed her idea of what to expect, leading her to believe that instead of a liberal arts school in Manhattan, she was actually bound for some version of an orgy interspersed with classes like "The Sociological Impact of Mercantilism in Western Europe: 1600–1750" (you know, practical, useful information that would directly impact and inform a later career). But she soon found that, despite having talked with plenty of current college students and having attended a relatively academically rigorous high school *and* reading guidebooks, she was unprepared. Beyond increased academic difficulty or new social situations, she was hardly prepared for even the most basic experience of *existing* at college in a structural way.

It didn't take too long after stepping on campus for Julie to basically have a panic attack. She was convinced that she was failing at life and began—to her abject horror—to long for her high school days. She hardly graduated high school as the prom queen, beloved by the student body whom teachers tearfully hugged goodbye, wondering if they should abdicate their professions having perfected the student–teacher relationship with her. (She was—not entirely inaccurately—known as the weirdo with a dark sense of humor. *C'est la vie.*)

Anna spent her entire adolescence believing that if she just made it through high school, karma would be on her side, and by the time freshman year rolled around, she'd be "cool in college." She came by this belief honestly: For years, every adult told her that all the things that made her weird and lonely (her obsessions with poetry, improv comedy, and guys in preppy indie bands) would suddenly translate into being hot and connected as soon as her feet touched down on her liberal arts college campus.

There was some truth to this belief—a few months into her freshman year, she had friends, the dining hall was friendly and welcoming, she got onto an improv troupe, and people saw it as an accomplishment. But inside, she still felt weird and scared, and everyone else seemed more okay with everything than she was. She had a creeping worry that everyone would discover that she wasn't as cool as she seemed, and she would end up feeling as alone as she had in high school. As time went on, she realized not only that everyone, to some extent, worries about being an outsider their freshman year but also that no one actually thought it was that cool that she made it onto an improv troupe to begin with.

She didn't miss high school, not even a tiny bit, but a part of her missed how structured things were then. In high school, she knew her teachers, what they expected from her, and how to do the work. She knew which mean girls to avoid. She could blame not going to things on her mom. In college, there was so much newness around her all of the time that she yearned for what was known. Okay, maybe she missed high school a tiny bit. But, like, don't tell anyone.

Here's the thing: Missing high school makes sense no matter how you felt about it at the time. Despite being a confusing time of self-discovery and growing pains (to put it mildly), high school is also undeniably straightforward. High school is highly segmented and chronological, dictated by deadlines and schedules. You go to school for six or seven hours a day, five days a week, week in and week out. The impressive consistency of this framework is diversified by notable events like Homecoming and Prom, academic benchmarks like regular quizzes and tests, and the glorious paradises that are high school summers. A student's high school experience is laid out before her and defined by concrete indicators of progress, either achieved or failed.

Dealing with college on the most basic level of existence is kind of a free-for-all. There's plenty of work—midterms, finals, papers, and lab reports abound (rejoice!). But, basically, your time is completely your own beyond the relatively few hours you spend in the classroom. Your schedule (and life) is an open book. Nobody at college—professors or fellow students alike—will check up on or in with you. Your parents may be only a motivational and encouraging text or call away, but that's different than the type of monitoring that probably used to incite endless eye-rolls and under-the-breath muttering in high school. You're on your own.

Most high school students look forward to this kind of freedom. And it's true: There are no curfews, no seemingly arbitrary rules, and, we won't lie, it's a limitlessness that can be incredibly empowering and plain awesome. But it's also easy for everything from how you should pragmatically spend your time to your overall purpose and life direction to become less clear without those benchmarks and segmented, prescribed time. It's a complex experience and one that can be deceptively challenging to navigate.

So, if college isn't *entirely* fun and games, then why are we so committed to projecting such an idealistic version of the experience? We think it starts at the very beginning of the college application process, especially when it comes to the idea of "fit" or that there is a single institution that's perfect for each prospective student. At some point during the past few decades, the whole college process became a veritable romantic comedy starring you (a terrified and/or somewhat apathetic high school student more concerned with passing the SATs than with the typical leading lady dilemma of saving your struggling cupcake bakery or boutique dog grooming shop) and the ivy-covered campus that is Your Perfect Fit (which is less a macho-yet-sensitive love interest than it is an inanimate object with a history of misogyny and institutional exclusion). The myth continues once you step foot on campus: You're supposed to lay your eyes on the University of Your Dreams (your Sexy Love Interest) and *know* that it just feels *right* and that you *belong*.

Here's the thing. This romantic narrative is far too black and white and (much like real rom-coms) wildly unrealistic. In this version of the story, there is one college that is Right For You that will ensure Perfect Happiness and a Great Future. But in reality, colleges are not fairytale resorts designed to hand students happiness and success in exchange for their tuition (although, based on tuition rates, it's not unreasonable to expect that that would be the case). Rather, the "college experience" is intimately shaped by who ends up attending the same school (and of those people, who ends up on your hall freshman year, who also writes for the school paper, etc.), which classes you get into, and which professors deign to enlighten the minds of undergraduates that semester.

Your college experience is going to be less about this mythic idea of "fit," less about the right college providing you with everything you need and leading you along a guided journey (like the prescribed high school experience) than it is going to be what *you* do with basic resources made available to you and the mindset with which you approach them. Ultimately, college is a dynamic experience in which *you are half the equation* and a hugely informative source of your own experience. It's not up to the college to hand you a great experience: You have to navigate your newfound freedom and fight for your own happiness.

MYTH: If you are struggling, you're the only one who is.
TRUTH: *Everybody* goes through a period of adjustment—there's just a weird culture of silence about maintaining the aforementioned idealistic illusions about college.

It took years for the truth about our freshman years to come out among my friends. During one Buzzfeed-trolling marathon (this was, of course, before TikTok) Julie's sophomore year, she started reminiscing about the previous year with her friends. One friend got straight to the point: "Did you guys also feel terrified and unprepared basically all the time? Or was that just me?" The entire group immediately erupted into a chorus of "Oh my god, yes" and "I definitely thought I was the only one failing at life." Across the country, almost ten years later, the same conversation took place with Anna's group of friends. We had all assumed we were the only ones who felt unprepared for a radically new and different experience, that we were completely alone in our social and academic struggles, and yet it wasn't until after the fact that we realized we had all had the same freshman experience—one that is probably far more common than not.

So why are we so committed to this silence? Well, it's hard to be the first one to speak. When everywhere you look, people are laughing or studying or walking to some cool destination you don't know about, it can feel like everyone else is having the most amazing time, so there isn't an incentive to be the first one to admit things are hard. In college (and to some extent in life), we all want to connect with others, but we don't want to be vulnerable, which is tricky because the only way to form true connections is to be vulnerable.

In fact, being vulnerable goes against everything society has trained us to be up until this point. The Hunger

Games-Sparta-fight-to-the-death hybrid that is the college admissions process certainly sets the tone for how we approach the entire experience. The independence, ruthless determination, and single-minded competition that the process requires breed isolation: We know there are only a limited number of spots for admission, so we get into a pattern of withholding information, of refusing to lend a helping hand. It's every woman for herself.

It's an attitude that's specifically ingrained in women beyond college, too: Young women are entering a workplace that still undeniably breeds gender discrimination. About four in ten women in the United States say they have faced discrimination while working because of their gender (Parker and Funk 2017). Women of color are particularly impacted: Research indicates that all women, but particularly women of color, still experience stifled leadership opportunities, the persistence of sexual harassment, and doubts about their competence, intelligence, and skills unrelated to their actual performance (Krivkovich et al. 2022). Consciously or not, many young women have watched their mothers and have deduced that the workplace (and, in many ways, society at large) is still not open to women the way it is to men. But instead of attacking the sexist system that produces such attitudes, women all too often attack and compete against each other for those limited spots. Instead of drawing strength from each other and learning from each other's mistakes, we continuously repeat them based on the idea that we must selfishly guard our own experiences because success for women is a limited resource. We make things unnecessarily difficult for ourselves and allow that power dynamic to persist.

It also doesn't help that young women are pressured to be perfect and never admit to any kind of failure in a way that young men simply are not. Starting as early as middle and high school but continuing and even intensifying in college, we're brainwashed to believe that we have to do really well in school, meet narrow definitions of beauty, and generally live up to, if not surpass, impossibly high standards. Socially, we have to manage insane double standards like being sexy yet chaste, smart but not smarter than the guys around us, etc.—standards that manifest in unique and increasingly stringent ways in college.

It's this kind of gender-based competition and perfectionism that keeps young women from admitting that they're struggling or not always having the best time. We interpret reaching out to each other, admitting our struggles, and offering a helping hand as showing weakness instead of as a potentially vital source and act of strength. But that *hardly* means women generally, as well as freshmen specifically, aren't all struggling. At some point, we all are.

But there is good news (thank God, right?). Although your freshman year, and college generally, can be a challenging time, it's also an incredible opportunity for women to confront these double standards and high expectations and take on the issues that women of previous generations have yet to solve, like work–life balance, "having it all," and beyond. With the right information and support on your side—like the kind offered in this book—you can make the next year, as well as the rest of your undergraduate experience, an amazing opportunity to set yourself up for a life full of authentic success and happiness.

We'll be honest: There are *few* other sources for real talk about how to handle something that is portrayed as the easiest time of your life but, deceptively, might be the hardest—and the most crucial. There are even fewer (if any) that take these issues on from the vantage point of a smart, driven woman. Julie looked for this kind of advice when she was about to head off to college and instead found a bunch of tomes filled with repetitive, self-evident, and ultimately unhelpful generic advice. *Don't tell me that I should get shower shoes before I leave; yes, that's actually a solid point, and I'm a tried-and-true warrior in the fight against foot fungus, but I know that.*

Tell me the real stuff! she thought while reading such disappointing guidebooks.

Well, here it is. You'll get unbiased facts and testimonials from young women who were just at college (and they're all anonymous and told us everything in confidence, so you *know* they're telling the truth). Basically, we'll destroy the idea that the college experience is a one-size-fits-all stereotype and allow you to claim your own unique, satisfying experience. Because while college is certainly about education, making a good investment in long-term financial security, and, yes, having fun, at the end of the day, it's about *your* life. And at the very end of the day, we live our lives in the pursuit of happiness, right? So why not start now?

REFERENCES

Krivkovich, Alexis, Wei Wei Liu, Hilary Nguyen, Ishanaa Rambachan, Nicole Robinson, Monne Williams, and Lareina Yee. 2022. "Women in the Workplace 2022." McKinsey & Company. www.mckinsey.com/featured-insights/diversity-and-inclusion/women-in-the-workplace.

Parker, Kim, and Cary Funk. 2017. "Gender Discrimination Comes in Many Forms for Today's Working Women." Pew Research Center. December 14. www.pewresearch.org/short-reads/2017/12/14/gender-discrimination-comes-in-many-forms-for-todays-working-women/.

CHAPTER 2

PREPARING FOR D-DAY

Getting Ready for Freshman Year (And How to Deal When It Actually Happens)

One of Julie's strongest memories from the summer before she left for college was cleaning out a closet full of about a decade's worth of accumulated junk. It took her the better part of a week to sort through an impressive array of stuffed animals, various trophies of participation given to all of the equally untalented athletes on her various elementary school teams, and every greeting card she'd ever been given.

To any other normal human being at any other time in her life, that hodgepodge of random items would be all but meaningless, but to her sentimental, nostalgic, recent high school graduate self, every single item evoked an emotionally charged memory. At some point, she ended up crumpled on her bedroom floor in despair, clutching a birthday card created on Microsoft Word 1998 (yes, she's that old) in Comic Sans font. "Marissa wrote me this for my 10th birthday," she sobbed, referring to what was obviously a hastily assembled birthday card from her best friend. "I WILL NEVER FIND ANOTHER FRIEND WHO UNDERSTANDS ME EVER AGAIN!"

DOI: 10.4324/9781003408932-2

Unlike Julie, Anna was ready to be surrounded by new people who didn't know her at all. For the past four years, she had bought into the myth that if she just made it through the sweaty hallways and treacherous social dynamics of high school, she'd get to be cool in college. In her mind, college was a magical place where she would no longer be heartbroken over her mediocre high school boyfriend or care that she wasn't included in any after-prom shenanigans. It was simple, really: She just needed to arrive and not be that weird during orientation, and everything she ever wanted would come true and she'd never feel awkward again. So, as summer went on, she attempted to shed her high school self and become the new version of herself—the one who would walk across campus with exactly the right music playing in her ears.

The months that hang between high school and college are seriously challenging. Some people (like Anna) feel they should prepare themselves for a new chapter by pulling away from their high school friends. Others (like Julie) experience extreme nostalgia and are more willing to forgive any negative memories about their childhood and high school in favor of an idealized view of the past. And then there's the strong contingent who hated their high school, hometown, and everything associated with both and are methodically counting down the days until they can escape. No matter how you feel, the bottom line is that being in a state of in between, in a drawn-out transition, is incredibly difficult.

And at the same time that you're dealing with all of those feelings, there's the very concrete reality of actually, physically getting ready for college. You're going to be on your own for the first time, and trying to anticipate what you'll need (not to mention what you'll *want*) as you break out on your own can be tricky.

But not to fear: We've got hindsight on our side. By the end of this chapter, you'll be so prepared for this transition that your resident assistant (RA) will probably (gladly) recruit you to lead your first floor meeting.

CONNECTING WITH OTHER STUDENTS

Even before you pack, one of the first things you'll likely do after enrolling in school is to join a class social media profile. When Anna and Julie were heading to college, they both joined class Facebook pages. Freshmen today, however, are more likely to follow or be followed by a class Instagram page. No matter the social media platform, though, the same anxieties and questions are likely to come up: Should you follow your future fellow freshmen first? Should you make your profile public if it's private? Should you attempt to completely rebrand and delete all evidence of who you were in high school?

The answer to all of these questions is actually kind of simple: As long as you're kind and conscious of basic manners, it won't matter that much what you do before you land on campus. In our experience, everyone whose reputation was determined by their pre-college social media behavior had acted in ways that made them negatively stand out. And you don't want to be "That Kid."

DON'T BE "THAT KID"

Almost without fail, one kid usually manages to single themself out on these group platforms. For Julie, it was a girl who thought it was a good idea to post multiple videos of her ranting to a group of complete strangers. The "That Kid" of a friend's class Facebook group was a guy who would post links to highly pretentious thought pieces and then pick fights with anybody who dared to disagree with his (extensively detailed) opinions about them.

Just remember that this is the very first impression your *entire* class will have of you—and it's amazing how, although most students can barely remember what their professor said five minutes ago, *everybody* seems to remember the kid who dominated their class's Facebook or Instagram page the summer before freshman year.

DON'T BE AFRAID TO POST, EITHER

That being said, this *is* your first chance to get to know your future fellow classmates. Although you probably shouldn't try to dominate the group or page or let your freak flag fly (wait until finals when the full range of human and even animal behavior is not just acceptable but expected), it's actually a good idea to reach out. Introduce yourself, mention some of the things you're passionate about, ask if somebody wants to attend a nearby concert—whatever you choose to write, just make yourself known. Finding somebody who shares an interest by reaching out to everybody all at once is far more efficient than engaging in a ton of individual conversations. Julie knew of people who found great friends due to a shared interest expressed on their class's Facebook page—people they might not have encountered otherwise.

Also, it's great to show up on campus with a plan to meet up with some people or to look out for somewhat familiar faces—it makes the transition that much easier. Just make sure you don't greet people as if you know them if you're only acquainted with them by surreptitiously viewing their profile without any real contact. It's an easy trap to fall into but a very creepy one.

DON'T JUDGE OTHERS BY THEIR POSTS

It's a pretty well-established fact that people almost always present themselves differently on social media than they do in person. Especially when introducing themselves to a ton of potential friends, kids often self-consciously rewrite their posts or comments multiple times until their true voice and thoughts are unrecognizable (or, conversely, don't think *enough* about how they're coming off to a ton of different people; i.e., "That Kid"). Don't allow a single post or profile to completely shape your view of an individual: Try to give them the benefit of the doubt.

WHAT DO I BRING?

There is one very basic rule you need to remember when packing for college: Do not—we repeat, do *not*—bring every worldly possession with you to school. In fact, you should bring the absolute minimal amount of material possessions possible. Although your first instinct might be to bring along things that remind you of home and offer some kind of comfort and familiarity, you may feel differently when you show up to your tiny dorm room. The truth is, being able to walk around your clutter-free room will be far more comforting than climbing over non-essential possessions that remind you of home.

But what qualifies as essential? Of course, it's ultimately up to you to know what you really need (and want) at school, but Figure 2.1 provides some basic guidelines.

WHAT TO PACK

1. Bedding
- **Bedsheets, Blankets, a Comforter, Pillow, and Pillowcase:** Thanks to almost every college's insistence on providing extra-long twin beds, which NOBODY ELSE EVER IN THE WORLD has, you likely won't be able to bring your own bedding because that would make too much sense.
- **A Mattress Pad:** Arguably less essential but it actually makes a huge difference. And in college, getting a good night's sleep is *always* a solid investment.

2. Room
- **Desk and/or Floor Lamp:** Fluorescent lights—the dorm room light of choice—act quicker than any kind of downer in pill form possibly could. Invest in soft/soothing/human-friendly lighting instead.
- **Alarm Clock:** A smartphone's alarm works just fine, but in case you want to double up on alarms before a final.
- **Power Strips:** There are never enough outlets. NEVER.
- **Kitchen Supplies:** Including plastic plates and dishware, nonperishable food like granola bars, and, for the real food-lovers out there, a mini fridge.

3. Toiletries
- **Towels:** Of the bath, wash, and hand variety.
- **Robe:** Unless you want to parade around in just a towel, then go ahead.
- **Hair Supplies:** Hair dryers/straighteners/curlers are handy.
- **Shower Caddy:** Full of the basics—shampoo, conditioner, you hopefully know the hygiene drill by now.
- **Shower Flip Flops:** Arguably the most essential thing for facing a communal, questionably sanitary shower.
- **Over-the-Counter and/or Prescription Meds:** Advil/Tylenol, cough drops, decongestants, Pepto Bismol—you will need all of them at some point.
- **First Aid Kit:** Including bandages, antiseptic cream, etc.—college is a war zone.

4. Technology
- **Laptop:** You likely already have one, but if you used your high school's computer lab or shared a family computer, seriously consider investing in a laptop. Although most schools have communal computer labs, laptops can be great for taking notes in class, writing papers, and access to endless mindless distractions. Many online marketplaces and even big-name stores offer student discounts.

FIGURE 2.1 WHAT TO PACK FOR YOUR DORM ROOM

- **Chargers (for Phone and Laptop):** If you have extras, bring those too.
- **Printer:** Most schools have printers available for students' use, but if you're a procrastinator who likes to print out papers without waiting in line or worrying about technical difficulties five minutes before class, consider bringing your own.

5. Clothing
- **Winter/Seasonal Clothes:** Coat, gloves, hat, winter boots if applicable.
- **Fancy Clothes:** Especially if you're planning on rushing a sorority, you'll need a dress for formal and other recruitment events.
- **Business Attire:** Your school will likely have a career fair or other professional events—don't show up in sweats. You're a semi-adult now, damnit.
- **Everyday Clothes:** Jeans and T-shirts are your friends.
- **Pajamas**: These double as everyday clothes after those first few weeks when you're no longer trying.
- **Shoes:** Less is more; generally you'll need athletic shoes, a good pair of heels, a nice pair of flats, sandals, and boots.
- **Bags:** Wristlets are always great for going out; bigger shoulder bags are great for carrying notebooks/books to class.
- **Jewelry:** Just don't bring anything too valuable.
- **Swimsuit:** If you like to do laps or if you go to a warm-climate school…lucky.
- **Workout Clothes:** Exercise is a huge stress release and is also pretty good for you
- **Sewing Kit:** For when you inevitably destroy something. It happens.
- **Laundry Supplies:** Hangers, detergent, laundry bag, stain removers like Tide To Go Pens, which are akin to a religious experience, and Downy wrinkle releaser or an iron/ironing board if you're old school.

6. School Supplies
- **Note-Taking Supplies:** If you don't plan to take notes on your computer, make sure you have the basics, including:
  o **Notebooks and Pens/Pencils:** Reacquaint yourself with your handwriting and give your prematurely arthritic fingers a break from typing.
  o **Sticky Notes:** These are so useful for studying, writing yourself reminders, or writing your sleeping roommate a note and leaving it on her forehead (LOL COLLEGE IS FUN!).
  o **Paper Clips, a Stapler, Scissors:** Basically any stationery material you feel you objectively don't need in the digital age but then *always* end up needing.

FIGURE 2.1 CONTINUED.

- **Calculator:** May the quantitative forces be with you.
- **Folders:** Organization is key. Keep track of various handouts, readings, and returned papers, and you'll be that much more prepared for finals—seriously, it makes a difference.

7. Miscellaneous Stuff
- **Important Papers:** Bank info, car registration, financial aid forms.
- **Important Cards:** Driver's license, credit cards, medical insurance card, Social Security card.
- **Dorm Survival Aids:** Earplugs (for when you have a 9 a.m. exam and your roommate does not), fan, flashlight, a duffel/overnight bag (for when you need to escape).
- **Umbrella:** Try to keep a small one with you in your bag—you will get caught in the rain when you're having an awesome hair day.
- **Beach Towels:** For sunbathing when you should be studying, plus for dealing with any number of disgusting dorm-related situations.

FIGURE 2.1 CONTINUED.

A DIFFERENT KIND OF "GIRLS GONE WILD": THE ROOMMATE

THE ROOMMATE ASSIGNMENT

Different schools handle the roommate assignment differently. Many allow you to request a roommate, most have the option of random matching, and some still require that you show up on move-in day without a clue about who will already be unpacking their stuff in your room. If you have the option to choose whether or not you want to pick your own roommate or undergo a random assignment, there are some pros and cons to consider, as noted in Table 2.1.

Table 2.1

The Roommate Assignment

	PROS	CONS
CHOOSING YOUR ROOMATE	Whether you choose to live with a friend from home or somebody you met at a new student's weekend or on social media, there's a degree of comfort in knowing at least some defining details about the person with whom you'll be sharing a room for a year. You can also coordinate purchases for the room, like a mini fridge (you know, the truly important things).	Especially if you choose to live with a close friend, you may be relegating yourself to your comfort zone *too* much. Although it's totally possible to branch out with your best friend at your side, feeling like you have to be the same person you've always been with her may make it hard to explore other aspects of yourself. Also, spending social *and* downtime with your best friend is a *lot* of time together. Chances are you'll begin to irritate each other, and the lack of space could actually harm your relationship.
RANDOM SELECTION	Your school is probably working off of some kind of survey you filled out, so you will likely have at least some lifestyle-based preferences in common with your roommate. As you'll find out, this may be more valuable than having actual interests in common: At the end of the day, you want to be comfortable and at peace in the place you live, not committed to a 24/7 sleepover.	You (and frankly, the people assigning you to your roommate) have no idea what this person is actually like. They could present themself one way on paper and turn out to be completely different. You just never know what you're going to get.

WHAT TO EXPECT WHEN YOU'RE EXPECTING...A ROOMMATE

It might be a universal (and perverse) hobby of college upper-classmen and graduates alike to terrify rising freshmen with cautionary roommate stories of horror. The summer before Julie's freshman year, it seemed like all she had to do was mention that she was about to start college, and the aforementioned upperclassmen and graduates would inquire about her roommate situation. Apparently, admitting that she didn't yet know her roommate was basically an invitation to terrify her with stories of the ill-adjusted human beings assigned to live with whomever she might have been talking to. So she was prepared for the worst.

She's happy to report that she did not get stuck with a sociopath. She never woke up to her roommate hovering above her bed, whispering, "I just like watching you sleep." Her roommate never hoarded insect-attracting stashes of food, didn't attempt to build a replica of Mount Everest out of her laundry, and never required her to dismiss "very special" visitors. They were never best friends but respected each other's space and requests, asked about each other's days, and occasionally shared amusing anecdotes.

Like many other rising freshmen girls, though, Anna and Julie had an idealized vision of what their roommate relationships would be like. They imagined long nights of plotting future world domination over jars of Nutella, living together every year, and then making time for weekly brunches post-graduation. That definitely didn't happen, but it turns out that having a courteous, respectful, and somewhat professional relationship with your roommate may actually be the ideal living situation. We know people who were instantaneous best friends with their roommates and then ended up fighting with them often, their relationship strained by *constant* exposure to each other. Constant interaction with *anybody*, even somebody you really like and care about, is a lot of work.

The Actual Rules You and Your Roommate Should Use to Make a Contract

Many RAs will require you and your roommate to make a formal contract outlining your ground rules for living together. Even if it's not required, though, it's absolutely a good idea to create an agreement anyway. You'll want something concrete to refer to if you and your roommate(s) get into an argument or situation. Don't be afraid to be brutally honest and advocate for your comfort: The standard questions about keeping the room clean and whether or not you're a night owl or early riser probably won't cut it. Here are some rules you might want to throw out there:

1. If you're in a long-distance relationship, please avoid marathon FaceTime sessions that last well into the early morning hours.
2. Please give me some notice if you plan on sexiling (exiling a roommate for the purpose of sex) me—*especially* if a long-distance partner is visiting for multiple days.
3. If you get back really late or get up really early and I'm asleep, please make every effort to be as quiet as possible.
4. Don't. Eat. My. Food.
5. Please engage in any and all illegal activity outside of the room (including drugs, alcohol, or the selling of either).
6. Rooms/suites should generally be clean. Let's figure out some type of chore wheel or fair way to address that.
7. You also need to clean yourself. If your body odor is the dominant scent in our living space, we have a problem.

The most common types of challenging roommates. And, of course, there are the roommates who necessitate some serious character-building. For dealing with *those* roommates, we can offer some advice.

TYPE 1

The Antisocial or Socially Awkward

I HAVE TOO MUCH WORK TO HANG OUT!

The situation. Whether it's because they have mistaken your room for the library and study 24/7 or because they're possibly agoraphobic, this roommate always gives you a hard time about having people over and never allows you any privacy. It's easy to roll your eyes at this roommate, complain about them to other friends, and label them a weirdo, but there are plenty of serious possible reasons driving their antisocial behavior. They may be putting so much pressure on themself to succeed academically that they can't handle being social. They may be painfully shy or even depressed. "Weird" shouldn't be the go-to assumption.

The solution. Reach out to them. It may feel counterintuitive if their rules and general presence are pissing you off, but oftentimes, the people who reject social interaction often need friends the most. Try to get to the bottom of why they're so opposed to socializing (in a noninvasive, respectful way, of course). If that doesn't work, just accept that they are who they are and try to respect their wishes. Definitely don't speak badly about them behind their back or alienate them further.

TYPE 2

The Bully

The situation. This roommate didn't get the memo that high school ended and thinks it's still permissible to make immature comments and be manipulative. Maybe they'll make a comment about how the Freshman 15 really affects *some* people more than others. Maybe they'll silently judge your outfits. They make your room into a passive or blatantly aggressive war zone.

The solution. It's never easy to rise above somebody's horrible behavior, especially if it's directed at you, but it's necessary to try. At the risk of sounding like your mother when you were in middle school, try talking it out. Be honest about how they're making you feel, ask them why they're behaving this way, and ask them to stop (like good adults are supposed to). If that doesn't work, try to be unfailingly nice to them despite their rudeness. Bullies thrive on evoking reactions from their victims: They want to get in a war with you because they feed off the drama, but you won't benefit from a fight; you'll just waste time and energy. Don't give in, but talk to your RA if things get really bad. If it's a truly unbearable situation, look into your school's room change policy.

TYPE 3

The "Slut"

The situation. First of all, it's really crappy to refer to other people, especially girls, as "sluts"—to make judgments about them based on their sexual practices and/or preferences. It's a sexist double standard to view women in particular negatively for expressing themselves sexually in a way that men are encouraged to. Women aren't doing themselves any favors by perpetuating these standards or by holding each other to ridiculous standards of "purity."

> Can you find **somewhere** else to sleep tonight?

That being said, it's one thing to generally support someone's right to sleep with whomever they want, whenever they want, and another to have to live in the place where they're doing that. You have a right to privacy and, beyond that, a right not to be greatly inconvenienced by their sexual exploration.

The solution. Again, don't call your roommate or anybody else a "slut" behind their back (or to their face, for that matter). It can be tempting to gossip about your roommate, especially when it's so encouraged in our culture, and especially if their behavior is making you uncomfortable or is annoying. Resist. Accept that if it does seem like they're genuinely having a good time sexually experimenting and liberating themself, that that is just a part of college for many people. However, it's also worth noting that if you get the sense that your roommate is being so sexually active out of insecurity, to prove something to themself, or for any other negative reasons, then you should try talking to them about it. Talking through their issues may prove to be a much more helpful coping mechanism for any type of trauma or other issues they might be trying to navigate.

But, as for you: You have a right to set boundaries (and the earlier you do so, the better). It can be awkward to talk about sex—especially with somebody you just met—but it's important to take a firm stance on hook-up rules right away for the sake of your long-term comfort. Write up a contract, and don't be afraid to confront them if they breach it.

TYPE 4

The Thief/Mooch

The situation. It's beyond obnoxious to come back to your room to find your stuff moved, missing, or broken. Beyond being incredibly frustrating and inconvenient, it's really unsettling to feel insecure about the safety of your possessions and to always feel like you have to be alert in what should be a safe, comforting space.

The solution. First and foremost, make it clear whether or not your roommate can access your stuff on the first day of school. If you didn't discuss those boundaries, you need to confront them as soon as you suspect they may be using or taking your things. Many people, afraid of conflict, notice their stuff is missing but refuse to confront their roommate about it. Of course, accusing somebody of being a thief is no small matter and shouldn't be done haphazardly, but if you're pretty sure your roommate is to blame, you *need* to talk to them.

There's obviously an ideal way to do this, and it's not to confront them as soon as they walk in the door and shout "THIEF! TO THE GALLOWS!" to your invisible army of enraged village people. First, ask if they "borrowed" your possessions. If they admit it, clearly request that they ask for permission to do so the next time or make it clear that your stuff is off limits. If they deny it, try to trust that they didn't, but if it's a reoccurring situation, present them with the evidence for your suspicions and lay down the law. If this pattern persists, get your RA involved. Although it would really suck to have to do this, if the situation does not abate, you may want to consider locking up your valuable stuff or switching rooms.

The same basic situation applies to mooches: If they're not stealing your stuff but borrowing a lot of it or generally relying on you for food or anything else, make it clear that true friendships are based on respect and reciprocation and that by mooching off of you, they're not demonstrating either.

TYPE 5

The Nonexistent Roommate

The situation. Especially if you don't get along, this situation can seem like a blessing at first: Your roommate is never around, and it basically feels like you have your own room— sweet freedom! But ultimately, it can be really disconcerting to have no idea where your roommate is. Every time they disappear, you have no idea if it's because they're staying with a friend, out of town, or lying in a ditch somewhere. Even if you're not close, you feel like you have some kind of obligation to alert somebody if they go missing...but don't want to overreact. It's a difficult balance.

The solution. When your roommate reappears, make sure everything is okay, and, if you think it will make you feel better, ask them to at least check in with a text letting you know they're alive. Beyond that, invest yourself in other things and be thankful you essentially ended up with a single at the double rate. If you start to get lonely, don't be afraid to keep your door open (if you live on a hall in a dorm) or invite friends over to hang out in your room or keep you company while you work.

I'll see you when I see you!

The bottom line is this: Whether you love or hate your roommate, having one at all will be a valuable life experience. Learning to live with somebody inevitably teaches you so much about yourself. You learn your limits and the boundaries of your patience, sure, but also self-awareness and the ability to compromise (ideally). At the very least, you get a few interesting stories out of it.

THAT DORM LIFE GRIND

We probably don't have to explicitly state this, but living in a dorm or any other type of communal living situation at college is *a lot* different than living at home. It's hard to say which is more disappointing: Finding out that the tooth fairy is a giant conspiracy perpetuated with an almost impressive dedication by the adult world or finding that there isn't a dorm fairy—that moving out really means you're living on your own. If your mom never made you do your own laundry, picked up after you, and nursed you back to health in sickness like ours did, then it's time for a harsh reality check. In college, when it comes to taking care of yourself and functioning in a basic way, you're on your own.

But, ironically, people also constantly surround you. In addition to your roommate, you'll likely live on a hall with a bunch of other people. Of course, all schools have pretty different living situations, but generally, freshmen are stuck in a basic configuration of living with a roommate (or roommates—hooray!) on a hall with a communal bathroom and possibly a kitchen or kitchenette. You'll likely be required to be on some type of full meal plan. It's the typical freshman living grind, and there are great things about it, as well as a few things that just have to be endured to put the rest of your life into perspective (or something).

LIVING WITH DUDES

Many dorms are coed—whether on the basis of alternating rooms or alternating floors. So unless you specifically request to live in all-women housing or go to a women's college or possibly even a religious university you'll probably be cohabitating with guys. This can lead to some interesting situations (especially if you're forced to share a bathroom, which can be somewhat traumatizing), including:

◇ **Running into half-naked guys on your hall:** Guys seem to generally have fewer inhibitions about their bodies (probably due to a media that simultaneously shames women about their bodies yet promotes sitcoms in which obese men still have gorgeous wives—just a hunch). Therefore, they tend not to take issue with walking to a coed bathroom in little more than a towel. Although this can sometimes be aesthetically pleasing, it can also be incredibly awkward.

◇ **Dealing with how *other* girls respond to those guys:** The presence of guys will inevitably cause girls in your dorm to act a little differently than they might in a single-sex dorm. For instance, there will always be girls who try to befriend the guys and act like a bro—the "pick me" girls. We can't say for sure *why* being friends with guys equates to coolness (or at least their perception of their coolness), but it probably has something to do with underlying sexist notions of men being superior, and thus, when they accept a woman's presence it makes her superior, too. Whatever, it's stupid. Also, there will certainly be girls scouting out their neighbors for convenient hook-ups (see the next section on "dormcest"), which can lead to awkward sexual tension as well as actual sex heard through very thin dorm room walls. Welcome to college.

◊ **Loud video games and music:** There probably isn't concrete data on this, but anecdotally, many girls confirm that guys are much more likely than girls to blast violent video games and/or music without any qualms about whether or not they are disturbing their neighbors. We could go into a gender-based rant about this, but we'll spare you and just advise you to buy earplugs.

◊ **Awesome guy friends:** Living with guys isn't all doom and gloom. It's ultimately another opportunity to forge unique and diverse friendships. Beyond pros and cons, friendships with guys tend to differ from those with girls, and variety is generally a positive thing.

The bottom line is that it's not easy to live in a common space with *anyone,* regardless of gender. Everyone just brings different strengths and weaknesses to the situation. The best way to approach communal living generally is to just keep an open mind: Try to befriend everyone, voice your issues calmly and with respect, and take up yoga, meditation, or some other mindfulness technique so that you don't actually lose it.

DORMCEST

"Dormcest" refers to hooking up with somebody who lives in your dorm. The convenience and accessibility of this arrangement make it an understandably enticing option, but there are some considerable downsides. If things don't go well (which, let's be honest, is usually the case), then it can make for an incredibly uncomfortable living situation, which just sucks. There's ample potential for awkward run-ins, blatant hostility, and even the possibility of running into your hook-up with their new partner—and that's just scraping the surface. Your room and dorm should generally be a place of refuge where you feel most comfortable, not somewhere you feel you need to avoid or tread carefully.

Our advice? Refrain from entering a romantic relationship with anybody in your dorm—in all cases, but *especially* if it's an intentionally casual relationship. Of course, if one of the residents of room 525 makes your heart flutter, your knees weak, and shares your passion for artisanal jam-making—go for it. We're all for true love, and, after all, you're a big girl and you can make your own decisions. Just beware that although relatively common, hooking up with somebody in your dorm has a high potential for making your life way more complicated than it has to be—and you already have bio homework for that.

MEAL PLANS

Many freshmen are required to be on a full meal plan for at least their first year. If that's the case, there's not a lot to say except if the food is bad, suck it up—it's just a year. If it's good, keep yourself in check. Your parents told you to eat your vegetables for a reason: If you only eat processed foods, you WILL BECOME ONE. Also, check out the chapter on wellness (Chapter 4) for tips about how to make nutritious choices on a meal plan (even in the most grease-soaked dining halls, it's possible to avoid becoming a moribund zombie, addicted to trans-fat and GMOs) and more on the weird dynamics of eating in college, especially as it relates to the way women tend to judge each other's food choices in really annoying and messed up ways.

It's also worth mentioning that dealing with the cafeteria dynamics required by being on a meal plan can feel a lot like being a high school freshman all over again. Before Julie left for college, she legitimately had nightmares about being the loner in the corner of the dining hall every single meal. In retrospect, it seems ridiculous, but the idea of eating alone freaked her out and seemed like the epitome of social failure. In reality, nobody cares if you eat alone—everybody is really busy, and most of the time, if you want to eat, it's necessary to fly solo. Also, it can be nice to have some alone time: In college, people surround you *all the time*. It can be nice to have a few minutes of peace and quiet while you savor what may or may not be meatloaf.

But, if silent meals aren't for you, don't be afraid to ask to join a table. One of the great things about college is that it's *not* high school. Chances are you won't be judged or turned away; you'll just give yourself another opportunity to meet new people.

AND SO IT BEGINS... BEING FRESHMEAT

We'll give it to you straight: Upperclassmen generally find freshmen annoying. In most cases, this is not a hostile opposition or an active form of continuous hazing but rather an impatience for their general newness. Our theory is that awkward, confused, and generally terrified freshmen often evoke upperclassmen's memories of their own awkward and confused freshman terror, and they're too busy to deal with feelings, so they channel those feelings into anti-freshmen sentiments. Or they're just jerks. It's definitely one of the two.

The best way to deal with these prevailing attitudes about freshmen is, first of all, to accept that they exist. They are unfair and often uncomfortable, but it's just generally how the hierarchy of college goes. Once you've accepted your relatively low status, own it. We don't mean to belittle yourself or treat yourself like you are lesser than anybody else due solely to your age and newness. That's bullshit.

What we mean by accepting your position is don't posture—don't pretend like you're anything other than what you are. Be humble. Ask for help. Don't act like you have all of the answers. It may seem like acting like you already fit in will help you adapt, but the opposite is actually true: People in general, as well as upper-classmen specifically, are much more amenable to those who are upfront about their shortcomings or about needing help rather than those who overcompensate.

However, you don't have to be completely clueless. It's amazing how little some college freshmen know when they step on campus when a lot of basic information—like where your classes are (get acquainted with a campus map, please) or the many functions of your student ID—is pretty easily accessible. Of course, it's not this kind of administrative information that rising freshmen are dying to know. It's the more subtle rules freshmen are usually clueless about: the emotions you'll have to navigate, the unspoken rules. That information is pretty hard to obtain from sources other than direct life experience, and every campus has its own cultural intricacies. But luckily, you have this book. We can't tell you exactly what you'll feel and face and how to navigate it, but here are some hints.

(DIS)ORIENTATION: BEYOND THE "INFORMATION GUIDE"

The bottom line of college orientation is that it's all about the paradox of feeling simultaneously comforted and entirely thrown off your axis, spinning rapidly toward the unknown. Or at least, that's what orientation was like for Julie and Anna.

For Julie, this paradox manifested itself at the very beginning of her "leaving-for-college journey" After posting her obligatory "Leaving for college. Thanks for the memories, everybody!" Facebook status, she packed all of her earthly belongings into the family car. That's when she realized that all of her earthly belongings *fit into the family car*. Although the reality of this totally satisfied the fatalist in her (so little materialistic baggage to weigh her down once the zombie apocalypse hits!), it also underscored the fact that the home she was leaving, the home she had grown up in and considered her own, really wasn't hers anymore. Statements she had made with confidence ever since clicking "submit" on her electronic application quickly turned to questions. This is what I want? I'm excited? I'm ready to be on my own?

But then she became immersed in Barnard's Orientation Program and got to know the campus and the incredible students that surrounded her. She felt somehow at peace, excited to start a new life. In fact, if she hadn't had to repeat her place of birth along with her name and intended major *every single time* she met somebody new, which was approximately every five minutes, she might even have temporarily forgotten about her home back in Ohio (but so it goes).

It hit Anna a few hours after her parents left her in her brand-new dorm room. The orientation activities were over for the day, and her roommate was nowhere to be found, so she wandered out of her room alone, looking to make some friends. As she walked, she realized that there was no one keeping track of where she was, and there was no time she had to be home by. For the first time, she felt entirely free (how exciting) and also entirely alone (how daunting).

Here's the thing about orientation: It might seem like an innocuous series of events where the people running it unfailingly smile in a way that never reaches their eyes (the hallmark of all bureaucratically planned and funded events), but it can actually be pretty emotional. You'll likely feel any or all of these emotions.

Homesick. For some who have never been away from home for long, who may have never left their hometown before, just physically going to college can be a really big deal. Being in a new town, a different state, or a completely unique subculture of the country can be a huge cultural adjustment for many people. It can be in small ways—a friend of Julie's from Arizona, for example, recalled complete bafflement about the boating shoes and cardigans that suddenly surrounded her when she arrived at Harvard—and in big ways, like feeling completely out of your element.

Even for those who have been away from home before, going to college can cause a unique type of homesickness. You know things will never be the same again: You'll just be visiting your childhood home, not living there (that is, unless you move back in with your parents after you graduate, which is the reality for many). You begin to long for not only familiar physical surroundings but also that *feeling* of home: You long for the feeling of being taken care of as much as you wish you lived in a place that didn't feel like a clinical institution (linoleum, cinderblocks, unidentifiable stains, and all).

Feeling homesick is totally and completely normal. Although it may feel like it will last forever at first, homesickness *will* subside. You'll soon be so busy—with school, new friends, and new opportunities—that you'll forget to miss home. And after some more time passes, school will even start to feel like home.

Euphoric. For extroverts, orientation will probably be a spectacular experience. You get to talk about yourself endlessly without seeming narcissistic, and it's one of the few times when social norms are acceptably suspended. How many times in life can you simply plunk yourself down at a table full of perfect strangers and put minimal effort into justifying your presence (a quip is preferable, but even "Chicken fingers are delicious. Am I right or am I right?" will suffice). Your peers, paralyzed by fear and the sheer newness of the situation, might silently judge you and make mental notes, but externally, they'll accept you. There are endless opportunities to meet *all* of the new people. Extroverts, this is your moment to shine. Enjoy.

Lonely. For all of the introverts out there, orientation can be a lonely, exhausting experience. The majority of the conversations you'll have during orientation will inevitably be superficial. When you're used to the kind of easy interactions that come from years of being around the same general group of people who understand (and accept) your quirks or even just have a working knowledge of your likes and dislikes, it can be really challenging to start from scratch.

Every time Julie talked with her best friends from high school during orientation, they had a common refrain: "Does anybody remember how to make friends?" She and her friends went to the same tiny school their entire lives, and it had been a long time since any of them had to find completely new people.

By the end of the first week of orientation, Anna was convinced that she had found the friends she had always dreamed of. Everyone was so open and friendly, and since she was invited to all orientation activities thrown by the school, she never felt excluded. She just had to show up, smile, and bam—a new friend. Of course, they were, for the most part, fluff friendships that either fell apart after orientation or simmered down into the occasional cross-quad wave. But at first it was easy to find people to go places with, and complaining about how stupid all the ice breakers were helped her bond with everyone. Those friendships were enough to help her make it to the first day of classes.

And that's an important distinction: There's a difference between finding and making "friends" and finding your "people." Friends aren't too difficult to come by—they're on your hall, in your classes, other members of a club. It's easy enough to talk and enjoy spending time with them. But your "people" are your non-biological family. They're the people you go to first with a problem and the ones you celebrate with when you meet someone special or get a great grade. Finding your people isn't always easy and is bound to take some time. Of course, there are always the stories of people who instantly connected with their freshman roommate the second they moved in or found their friend soul mate during their first hall meeting. More likely than not, it's going to take a little more scouring than that. But the key to remember is that you have to get through the somewhat false non-friendships, the incessant shallow conversations, to allow the real ones to emerge. And emerge they will.

Annoyed. Icebreakers, information sessions about how to best plan for your future academic experience, and mandatory viewings of fire safety videos can be the worst. Although there may be some fun activities planned and good times to be had during orientation, there's always the necessary crappy part—the guidelines, the housekeeping, the administrative information. Basically, you just need to grin and bear it. Make a mental note to help run orientation later on so that you can make fun of the freshmen who will have to do the same thing when you're a smug, informed upperclassman—it makes the whole thing somewhat more tolerable.

Embarrassed. Chances are there will be some parties on campus during your orientation period. And not the organized activities the college has sanctioned for you that feel more like a middle school dance than an actual collegiate social experience, but the kinds that involve prohibited libations. A word to the wise: A party during orientation is not the time to drink excessive amounts (especially if it's your first time drinking at all) or to generally exceed your limits in any big way. Stay alert and watch out for yourself and others. Although there may not necessarily be "reputations" on most college campuses the way there are in high school, orientation is still more like high school in that everybody is hyperaware of everybody else. Everyone feels super self-conscious and will gleefully grab any opportunity to point out other people's faux pas in the hopes of deflecting their own. Not to mention, this will be everybody's first impression of each other, and first impressions are not only pretty important but also hard to make up for.

Although we'll talk about partying, alcohol, and drugs in depth later in this book, note that orientation is not the ideal time to start testing your limits; there will be plenty of time for that later on. During orientation, just stay alert. Also, help out those who weren't given such advice. They'll (hopefully) thank you and remember that you were there for them, which could come in handy down the line—not to mention that it's just the right thing to do.

Luckily, orientation lasts for a finite period of time. Before you know it, school will be in full swing. Upperclassmen will swarm the campus, ready to get back into their routines. And although it can feel pretty overwhelming to still feel like you're desperately doggy paddling while everyone else is swimming with Olympic speed and agility, it's all about perspective: Try not to view the transition into the true start of college as an attempt to melt into the stream but as your first chance to truly emerge.

COLLEGE ISN'T A TIME OF "REINVENTION": IT'S ONE OF FREEDOM

There's a pretty pervasive myth that college is an opportunity for self-invention, that it's the best opportunity to reinvent yourself as the person you've always wanted to be. The idea is that shedding the skin of your high school self and designing a completely new one will allow you to be the best, happiest version of yourself—self-fulfillment *taken care of.*

But that presentation is seriously problematic. The idea that some manufactured version of yourself (based on media cues or on what you think other "successful" women are like) will make you happy seems pretty false. There are undoubtedly countless ways to define happiness, and those definitions have probably all been embroidered on an abundance of throw pillows around the world. But at its core, personal happiness is based on being well acquainted and comfortable with your *true* self—not a version of yourself cultivated from a variety of sources, including that perfect girl in high school that you'd totally hate if she weren't so damn lovable plus a Manic Pixie Dream Girl impression with a little bit of perfectly awkward and quirky Jenna Ortega candidness thrown in.

Impersonating the person you *think* you want to be won't make you happy because you'll constantly be performing, not living. It's only from the security produced by a strong sense of self that we can ever hope to know what will make us happy, let alone how to go after it—not from inventing a totally new character to play. The problem is not that young women need to find a place where they can invent a new, seemingly better persona. It's that many of us *don't* authentically know who we are.

While finding one's identity isn't necessarily a gendered issue, it definitely impacts women in a uniquely intense way. Applying and going to college may very well be the first time young women are asked to invest in themselves—to make a choice that will benefit them and revolves around their own self-fulfillment.

So, despite the popular theory that college is *the* opportunity to invent a new persona for ourselves because of a more externally accepting environment, college can actually be an environment that facilitates the first real opportunity to get to know who we've *always* been but have been encouraged to repress. By becoming acquainted with that true self and establishing an identity complete with self-confidence, self-esteem, and assertiveness, we will feel secure and know where we will best fit and how we can make the most out of our college experience.

And luckily, college is *full* of opportunities to allow ourselves to figure out who we are. Here are just a few ways you can embrace this opportunity

Try something you're afraid you'll be horrible at. Have you always loved singing, but only to the audience of your shampoo and showerhead? Have you always had strong opinions but a fear of public speaking? Now is seriously one of your last chances to truly explore a hidden talent or unexplored interest. Any adult will tell you that once you're a "real person" with a "real job," it becomes infinitely more difficult to pursue such things. And who knows? You could get involved with something that changes your life—whether it changes the course of your study, shapes your social life, or just makes you feel fulfilled and happy, you wouldn't be the first person to be positively impacted by embracing the possibility of failure. Also, try to embrace fear whenever possible. If doing something terrifies you, it's one of the best reasons to pursue it. One of the things you'll likely find in college is that everything is at your fingertips if only you embrace fear and gather the courage to reach for it.

Speak your mind. During Julie's entire first semester of freshman year, she was too terrified to speak up in any of her classes. She was worried that her peers would judge what she was saying and think it wasn't insightful enough. She was hyperaware of her freshman status and assumed that upperclassmen had access to a wealth of knowledge that a lowly freshman like her couldn't comprehend and shouldn't challenge by speaking.

In retrospect, holding herself back from speaking was ridiculous. When she finally started speaking in her seminar classes, she never embarrassed herself; she just benefited from contributing to a discussion, which, it turns out, is a really valuable part of your education. She also realized there wasn't any blinking neon sign following her around, demarcating her freshman status—her comments and presence in class were taken at face value. A college education is not about sitting lifelessly in a lecture, alternating between taking notes and online shopping. It's about engaging. And that sounds like very official textbook advice, but it's so true: You gain so much more by actively participating in your classes—it's the difference between being taught and *learning*. Also, being able to offer your opinion and speak in front of a group are *really* vital life skills—they'll be relevant and hugely important to whatever work you end up doing.

Befriend somebody you don't think you'll get along with. It's so easy to relegate yourself to hanging out with the same type of people you did in high school: If you're a theater person, it's easy to gravitate toward other people in the drama program; if you're an environmentalist, there are undoubtedly countless eco-enthusiasts ready to reach out to you. But college campuses are full of passionate students with unique talents and great intellect. Make it your personal mission to find somebody radically different from yourself and befriend them. Although it's great to find people who understand you and can relate to you in a specific way, it's also vitally important to meet people who can expose you to completely different perspectives and values. Maybe the friendship will work in the long term, and maybe it won't, but it will definitely be a valuable experience in some way.

We can't tell you exactly what to do to establish your personal identity, but we will encourage you to try some of the aforementioned things so you can figure out who the hell you are. Our society does a good enough job of actively objectifying and sexualizing women and breeding us to believe that there is no deeper self to invest in beyond our bodies, which only exist to please and/or attract men, without us giving in and helping them. And what better venue to try to figure this out than one that's pretty forgiving and full of a bunch of diverse options and influencing forces, both academic and social?

BEING PART OF A MARGINALIZED GROUP

But what if there are parts of your identity about which you are *very* sure and proud? How can you fully maintain these qualities, especially if they qualify you as a minority on your campus? For example, how can you embrace your identity as a Black woman on a predominately White campus? How can you maintain your Jewish faith on a predominately Christian campus? Especially in the face of others' ignorance (which, unfortunately, still often persists even in supposedly "enlightened" academic spaces), how can you proudly express part of yourself that makes you somewhat different from the campus majority?

First and foremost, try to find an already established group of people who share your identity. Chapter 6 discusses cultural sororities, which offer ethnically and culturally specific social communities. Most campuses have LGBTQ-oriented clubs and/or a Gay–Straight Alliance Club, as well as Hillel (a Jewish-based organization) and many other faith-based organizations. These various groups can be a great way to maintain your ethnic/religious/cultural identity within the context of a campus in which that identity is marginalized. If a specific group that caters to your identity or values doesn't exist, start your own! If your college's admissions officers are at least baseline adequate at their jobs, you will not be the only person of your ethnic/religious/cultural group on campus, and therefore will likely be able to find others interested in joining forces with you.

But beyond finding a support system, it can be really difficult to deal with being part of a marginalized community on an individual, everyday level—and there's no prescription for how to navigate that experience.

On Being Part of a Marginalized Group

I experienced more antisemitism once I reached college than I had my whole life. I think the best advice I can give is to never ever compromise who you are. Your identity is something you should be proud of, so try not to internalize the hate from people who try to shame you for it. It makes you stronger and puts you in a better position to fight these instances outside of college.

—Grace, Columbia College Chicago

When I started my college career, the first thing I noticed was that there were significantly fewer people of color, and even fewer women of color, in my classes than there were White students. This was intimidating because I felt favoritism was being shown toward my classmates who were White, and it made me nervous to speak up in my classes. However, the more I dared myself to speak up, the easier it became to feel like what I had to say mattered.

—Neha, University of Texas at Austin

I'm LGBTQ, and college has actually helped me deal with that. Christian high school was not the optimal setting to accept that, but I got involved with my university's GSA (Gay–Straight Alliance), and just knowing people who'd already been through this and interacting with them in person, rather than just online, helped me figure out how I wanted to make this a part of my life and integrate it into my self-expression. I'm active in the community of LGBTQ people at my university, and it all works because I've done it the way that feels most comfortable for me.

—Susan, Case Western Reserve University

The first few weeks (or even the entire first semester) of college can be legitimately scary. You'll probably struggle to figure out how you fit in—whether it's trying to find what makes you unique or preserving what you know makes you different. But rather than letting these feelings overwhelm you, remember that college is ultimately a time of freedom. It can be difficult to let go of the person you've always tried to be, especially if you have no idea who you really are beneath that. It can be frustrating to try to fight to maintain aspects of your identity that set you apart. But persist because becoming truly secure with your authentic self means setting yourself up for a life full of authentic self-fulfillment. It will lead to what *you* want, not what everybody has always told you to want. Don't let this opportunity pass you by.

CHAPTER 3

ACADEMICS

(Oh, Right, College Is Also About Learning and Stuff)

An essential part of the college experience is certainly what you learn outside of the classroom (like deep universal truths about humanity and how to cook all of your meals using just a mug and a microwave—you know, the *truly* important stuff). But, believe it or not, what you learn in the classroom is also pretty valuable. So what *really* goes on in those classes?

When talking about college, we often take for granted the idea that school is school. It's acknowledged that college classes will inevitably be harder than high school classes, but it seems to be assumed that academic success in college is a matter of inherent intelligence, of pushing yourself harder if you're struggling. But, like literally every other aspect of college, we're here to tell you that that's not quite the case—collegiate academics are not so cut and dried. But have no fear; there are definitely some tips and tricks that make academic success achievable for *everyone*, no matter what your grades were in high school and no matter how rough the transition to undergrad may feel at first.

 DOI: 10.4324/9781003408932-3

HOW COLLEGE IS ACADEMICALLY DIFFERENT THAN HIGH SCHOOL

At first, the idea of taking college classes might seem incredibly intimidating. Admittedly, that fear is rooted in some fact. For many (if not most) freshmen, the increased academic rigor of college classes can be a rude awakening. Of course, the extent to which academics are emphasized and the difficulty of classes will probably vary based on what school you attend, but no matter where you go, you *will be* enrolled in classes (shocking, I know), and you will be given the opportunity to strive toward a greater plane of enlightenment. For all of the lip service paid to college rankings during the application process, the ultimate truth is that your college education is largely about what *you* put into it. You can get a great education no matter where you go—that is, if you want and actively work for that education. With the exception of perhaps a few prerequisite or really basic 101 classes, college classes overall *will* be harder than those you had in high school—in myriad and distinct ways, including those discussed below.

DIFFERENT CLASS STRUCTURE

IN HIGH SCHOOL

Unless you went to some alternative Montessori school where you focused on being a global citizen through goat farming and meditation, you were likely enrolled in the same basic classes the entire year. For six or seven hours a day, five days a week, you went from class to class or an extracurricular or study period. Adults scheduled your life for you because everybody assumed (arguably not entirely incorrectly) that if left to their own devices, adolescent students would accomplish nothing. Teachers often kindly wrote key terms and other concepts on the board and varied the class with discussions, worksheets, and group work they learned about at those conferences they'd go to (that's likely where they were while you zoned out as soon as your substitute play a semi-relevant video). You were probably evaluated frequently: A test at the end of every completed textbook chapter and a paper due every time you finished a book. *When will it end?* you probably wondered, futilely slamming your head against your chemistry textbook. *Suck it up, Hester, you may or may not have muttered under your breath while reading The Scarlet Letter. Angry, sexually repressed Puritans are nothing compared to my AP Lit teacher, who may or may not be Satan in a wig and polyester blend sweater.*

IN COLLEGE

There are quite a few ways college classes are structurally different from those you took in high school. These changes (which often throw freshmen for a loop) include:

◊ **Less class time, more material covered:** You'll spend far less time in class yet cover way more material. A typical, standard-credit college class will probably meet for about a total of three hours a week (of course, with variation) and will also involve moving through material more quickly than you did in high school. This is why it's important to keep up with your work: Miss an assignment, miss a lot.

◊ **Different note-taking:** Of course, the academic world is not yet rid of lazy professors who just read off of their PowerPoints, but more likely than not, you'll have to devise a structured way of taking notes from a free-form lecture and distinguishing key points and concepts from the professor's narrative presentation of material. If you are enrolled in large lecture classes, you may also have a discussion section, in which you usually meet with a TA (teacher's assistant) in smaller groups to talk about the reading and class material in more depth. These discussions, although important, don't easily lend themselves to note-taking either.

◇ **More infrequent testing:** Many classes only have a mid-term and final; others only have a final paper (with, *of course*, a ton of variation). But there is a downside to infrequent evaluations: They count for large chunks of your entire grade. There are also usually no opportunities for extra credit, and few professors will let you make up any work or evaluations you miss. Also, because you are evaluated infrequently, between everything you had to read and the material covered in class, exams will likely cover a *ton* of information. So fewer actual assessments, much more material to cover, and intensified pressure to do well on those assessments.

INCREASED WORKLOAD AND EXPECTATIONS

IN HIGH SCHOOL

Remember groaning about *all the work* you had and how you were going to have to pull an all-nighter and "OH, THE INHUMANITY!" Well, you're about to wish you could travel back in time to stand face-to-face with your high school self whose teacher gave her study guides before tests, who knew exactly what to take notes on, and was tested on a chapter-by-chapter basis or assigned papers after spending a significant amount of time reading one book, and slap her in the face and tell her to stop whining.

IN COLLEGE

You may only have about three hours of class a week, but that hardly requires three hours of *work* a week. Spending two to three hours studying or reading outside of class for every hour of class time is pretty typical. Most of your work will be done on your own time, and doing it will be up to your discretion. It will also require you to take everything to the next level. Yes or no answers no longer apply—in fact, there are no longer yes or no questions to be answered: It's all about considering the "why." When writing papers, you'll have to back up your arguable claim (also known as a thesis) with evidence. You'll have to consider the possible counterarguments to your claim. You'll have to connect your ideas to other concepts and themes. This can be difficult for students who never had to challenge themselves in this way in high school. But, like everything, it's all about practice: If you struggle with writing a paper like this at first, it's most likely because it's new to you, not because you're not smart enough to get the hang of it.

INCREASED RESPONSIBILITIES

IN HIGH SCHOOL

Your teachers, classmates, and parents knew whether or not you were present in your classes. You might have gotten away with skipping a class every once in a while (SHAME!), but there was no way you could just not show up to class for the bulk of the semester. People invested in keeping you accountable to your education and unafraid to enforce their power surrounded you.

IN COLLEGE

You could hypothetically never go to class. Of course, your absence will be noted in the types of classes that *do* take attendance (discussion sections and smaller seminar classes), but especially in large lectures, it's unlikely that attendance will be taken. You are the only person accountable for making sure you get to class, and that freedom can be tempting. Nobody is going to wake you up when you inevitably press snooze 80 times before that heinous 9 a.m. class you didn't even want to take anyway (*the universe is so cruel*) and force you to go to class. Nobody is going to suggest you stop scrolling through Instagram for photographic signs that your social life is better than your high school arch nemesis's or gently remind you that online shopping is probably not the best use of your time. Preparing for your classes and exams and attending those classes at all are your responsibility. There is no handholding in college. There are no parents to tell you to quit wasting time. Your professors will probably not reach out to you if you're struggling. But then again, so it goes with life. Nobody is going to encourage you to put in the extra effort at work to get that promotion. Nobody is going to serve you helpful resources on a platter. Welcome to the world of adult accountability. There may be people available to help you achieve success, but it's ultimately your responsibility to motivate yourself to reach out to *them* and encourage *yourself to* be the best possible version of yourself.

So, yes, college is more academically challenging than high school. But, as it turns out, incoming college freshmen usually don't struggle academically because they're not intelligent enough to handle the content of college classes. More often than not, it's the somewhat intangible challenges of college classes that trip up new students. But luckily, there are plenty of ways to overcome the unique structural and organizational aspects of accomplishing collegiate work.

NOT TO FEAR! SUCCESS IS POSSIBLE

HOW TO GET HELP

This may seem like a somewhat bleak picture of a life of complete independence, but there are ways to deal with a new, challenging academic reality beyond sucking it up and realizing life is completely about self-reliance. Yes, you'll have to experiment, practice, and figure out what works best for you. But there are also various resources and individuals you can reach out to that will be willing to help you help yourself, including:

◇ **WHOM to ask for help:**
- *Your advisor.* You'll likely be assigned an academic advisor (either randomly or based on an indicated major preference) at the beginning of your freshman year. Advisors are a great initial resource. Their job is to guide your quest to becoming an independent and functional student. They are there to advise you on designing a schedule and refer you to other resources at your school if you need help beyond their abilities.

☛ *A specific professor.* Chances are, you will develop an academic crush on one or more of your professors. Beyond physical attractiveness, this could also easily be spurred by their dreamy use of words like "epistemological" and "acculturation" without blinking and how they cause your entire worldview to implode in an hour and a half or less. That's some straight-up, weak-in-the-knees brain-sexiness. Don't be afraid to get to know such a particularly talented professor. Visit during office hours, ask probing questions about lectures, and challenge the points he or she made—professors love it. If you take the time to let your professors know they're succeeding at inciting you to think, not only will your grade likely improve, but also you'll genuinely get a lot out of your conversation. These one-on-one conversations may inspire a great paper topic or help you better understand the class material on a deeper level. Also—side note—many scholarships, study abroad programs, and graduate school applications require a professor recommendation letter. On a more strategic level, you'll want to develop a good relationship with at least one or two professors so when the time comes, you can turn to them for a really great rec letter.

◇ **WHERE to get help:** One of the best-kept secrets on most college campuses is the truly copious resources available to students—both academic and health-related (we'll get into the latter in another chapter). Usually, colleges bury information about these resources in some giant information packet for incoming freshmen that nobody reads except for maybe your mom. It turns out your campus may have/ probably has:

- *A math and/or writing center.* These centers are often run by particularly gifted students at your college—usually upperclassmen—who are just *waiting* to help students develop a paper topic or demystify the way your math professor seems to be speaking English even though everything he or she says is completely incomprehensible. If you're struggling to write a paper or get through a problem set, these are *amazing* resources to have, and yet most students choose to struggle alone rather than to basically ensure a boosted grade and a better understanding of their academic material. Go figure.
- *A tutoring program.* Many colleges have tutoring programs that cater to areas more specific than the basic reading, writing, and arithmetic.

Tutoring isn't solely a freshman prerogative, either: Many upperclassmen seek out tutors for anything from economics to Spanish to computer science. Basically, there's no shame in asking

OUT OF THE MOUTHS OF ~~BABES~~ CURRENT COLLEGE STUDENTS

Academic Success

Being a great student comes from reading as much as you can and holistically becoming a person who is inclined to think deeply about things. That's a muscle that you have to train, so I read everything and started reading everything twice and annotating. It takes a lot of time, but I have noticed a profound change in who I am since I started reading more. So I would say do what feels optional and make it mandatory for yourself.

—Flynn, Brown University

for help. There's no such thing as a subject that's "too easy" to seek help for, and you're never "too old" to need a helping hand. These resources exist for everybody for any reason—take advantage of them.

HOW TO STUDY

It's kind of weird that even starting in middle and high school, it's assumed that students inherently know how to study in a way best suited to their particular learning style. The truth is that knowing how to study is an individualized skill that is hardly self-evident to most people. Figuring out how to study best is largely a process of trial and error—of trying different methods and seeing how you best process and remember information. But if you're at a complete loss, here are some general places to start:

◇ **WHOM to study with:** Studying in groups is a great way to process and remember information. Other students may raise questions or interesting points about the information that may not have occurred to you, or they may be able to explain concepts in a way that resonates with you better than the way your professor did. Even explaining a concept to another student helps you better remember and understand it. Also, it's just a way to mix things up: Sitting alone with a book in your lap for hours on end is not only boring and depressing but also can be ineffective after a while. Your mind is bound to wander, and at some point, you're just wasting your time.

◇ **WHAT to study:** Between your reading, lecture notes, and discussion sections, you're going to end up with *way* more information available to study than you'll be tested on. Before you start studying in earnest, it can be helpful to go through all of these notes and highlight or write out separately key points or other things most likely to be on the test so you're only focusing on the essentials. Knowing what information is essential often takes practice, though. It's a delicate, ever-changing balance of generally knowing what information you felt was key and what information your professor emphasized. There is no formula: Trust your intuition and dive in.

◊ **WHEN to study:** Cramming is definitely not the best way to study, yet it's often the default option for super busy college students. Do yourself a favor and at least *attempt* to start studying for exams a week or at least a few days before D-Day. If you break up all of the material you need to cover over a few days, it will inevitably seem more manageable, and you'll be more likely to truly understand and remember it all. You'll also leave yourself time to email professors and/or TAs or (better yet) visit their office hours and ask them questions in person. If you do go the cramming route, know your limits and give your mind some breaks—it's really not effective to study for hours on end. You're much more likely to benefit from studying for an hour and a half or so at a time with 15-minute breaks in between. Those breaks work as great incentives to get through your material. Also, showing up to a test after eight hours of sleep and digesting a well-rounded breakfast is much more valuable than showing up to a test with eight hours of studying and 47 cups of coffee under your belt.

◊ **WHERE to study:** Try to figure out early in the semester where you work and concentrate the best. Some people have to be in a silent library, others prefer coffee shops with a low level of din, and others don't see the point in putting in the effort to look like a human (valid) and never leave their dorm rooms. Don't take for granted that wherever your friends are studying is the best place for you—experiment a little with different locations. You might be surprised to find that after weeks of following your friends to the library, you're actually much more comfortable in the student center, or you might discover that if you keep showing up to the same Starbucks, sometimes they'll throw you a free refill out of pity for your greasy, unwashed, and distressed state (which is *obviously* not something we know from experience).

◊ **WHY study:** There are, of course, college students who choose not to study at all. But here's the thing: On some level, you have to ask yourself what the hell you're doing at college if it's not ultimately to learn. There is, of course, a strong case to make for having fun (all work and no play and whatnot). But it would be a real shame to graduate from college and find that when given amazing academic resources and a real opportunity to enlighten and push yourself, you just slacked off and wasted your time. Basically, get it together, and don't mess up this small window to open your mind in a really valuable way.

At the end of the day, academic success is a matter of trial and error, of figuring out what works for you. Your first semester of college may result in grades below what you were used to in high school. This is *normal* and even a common experience. Transitioning from high school to college is just that: a *transition*. Everybody takes time to adjust to new expectations and responsibilities. If you feel like you are making a genuine effort to learn how to prioritize and manage your work, trying out strategies that work best for you in terms of the amount of time and effort you need to put into readings and assignments, and seeking help in the areas that challenge you most, then you're right on track, no matter what your transcript says.

The best way to succeed academically during your first semester is to recognize and accept that you can't do everything perfectly— really ever, but especially not at the very beginning of this new chapter of your life. You need to cut yourself some slack while at the same time avoiding the mindset that you're doomed to fail, so why bother caring or trying. There's a way to not kill yourself trying to succeed while still putting in a solid and responsible effort—it's just up to you to figure out what that is.

THE BEAUTY OF ORGANIZATION

Some people do not see the iridescent beauty that is a well-organized life. To those who do: Well, our Type A sisters, we salute you. To those who don't: Let us try to show you the light. Having a well-organized life will not only make everything easier but also may very well make your academic experience more efficient. Here are some organizational tips:

◊ **Develop a filing system:** You'll likely have syllabi, handouts, and a ton of supplemental readings in addition to your textbooks or other assigned books for each class. Make sure you have a folder (digital or tangible) to file all of those materials (which you *always* end up needing to refer to or study again at some point) instead of letting them fall loosely away into the ether of your hard drive or dorm room.

◊ **Use a planner/calendar:** This seems very Type A, and maybe it is, but actually documenting everything that you need to do makes accomplishing it all seem infinitely more manageable. Buy an old-school planner, use the majestic miracle that is Google Calendar, or develop an intricate sticky note system—no matter how you do it, itemize your life. Having everything laid out before you keeps all of your obligations relevant and keeps you from forgetting about each item altogether.

◊ **Embrace organizational technology:** There are so many apps out there that can help you organize your life. Some favorites include Google Drive (upload all your work here so you know it's in a safe place!); Calendly (which helps you set up your schedule and determine when all members of a group can meet); Notion (a customizable online planner and note-taking site); and Mint (which simplifies your financial life by syncing your checking, savings, and credit card accounts and breaks down your spending into a budget).

THINKING AHEAD: PLANNING YOUR ACADEMIC CAREER

Talk to any college senior about her college experience, and most are likely to say something like, "It just went by so fast." You might then catch a wistful sigh and a glimmer of a tear in her eye as she considers the harsh reality of adulthood into which she is about to jump headfirst. But it's true: College does go by *so fast*. So, although you should take freshman year as it comes and don't need to enter college with a set idea of what you want to study or what you hope to accomplish in concrete terms, it's worth thinking ahead at least a little bit as you *will* need to make decisions—and the time to do so will arrive before you know it. From picking the first classes you'll take to thinking about what major you might want to declare down the line, it's all worth considering (if on a somewhat noncommittal basis) before you dive in headfirst.

CHOOSING YOUR CLASSES

Every school has a different approach to how incoming freshmen determine which classes they'll take. Some schools don't let students enroll until they arrive on campus. Others send out information about classes—including classes specifically recommended for freshmen—over the summer and require that you select your classes at that point. Whatever the timing or method of class selection your school employs, here are some universal things to keep in mind as you select your courses:

◊ **Take it easy:** There will be plenty of time to challenge yourself in the coming years. Your first semester is not the time to try to get into several labs and senior seminars. It might be especially hard for those overachievers used to piling on the AP classes to take a step back but remember: You're going to face a ton of new experiences and challenges in your first few months at school. You'll want to be able to devote a significant amount of time to all of these new experiences rather than be solely consumed by school. Don't slack off by any means, but be realistic about your course load (edging on the side of prudence).

◊ **Consider knocking out some general education requirements:** If you have no idea what classes to take, getting pesky requirements out of the way is a great place to start. For example, Julie attended Barnard College, which had the "Nine Ways of Knowing," which, despite the deceptive nomenclature, is not the title of a biologically ignorant Greco-Roman philosophy of human nature, but rather a set of requirements Barnard students were required to complete before graduating. Many Barnard students majoring in the humanities tried to end the evil hold that numbers have over their lives by knocking out the math- and science-related requirements right away, whereas the pre-med kids tackled classes in the domains of literature or "Cultures in Comparison" so they could focus on figuring out how to save other humans' lives and stuff.

◇ **Try to get into the class of a beloved professor:** There are plenty of sites out there that rate professors (like http://ratemyprofessors.com as well as university-specific sites). If you don't know what subject you might be interested in, signing up for a class with a really great, inspiring professor is as good a place as any to start. In fact, it's common knowledge among most college students that (generally) a professor is a much better indicator of whether or not you'll enjoy a class than the subject matter: A great professor can make anything interesting, whereas a horrible professor can make an interesting topic intolerable.

◇ **Think ahead toward your major:** There is no need to declare your major your freshman year. In fact, you should keep an open mind and explore classes in multiple areas that pique your interest to get a taste of everything that's out there before you make any decisions. However, if you are considering a pre-professional track, sometimes, in order to graduate on time, you'll have to start pretty much right away. In that case, you'll want to sign up for your labs and whatnot immediately so you don't fall behind in an already rigorous academic course. And speaking of thinking about your major...

Making Academic Choices

There's so much pressure to choose a major or choose a life path and stick to it, but there are so many people in the world that get out of college and get an awesome job and don't use their degree at all. So, I've been trying to stay on the path of what interests me and surrounding myself with people I want to spend time with and want to learn from.

—Julia, University of Michigan

CHOOSING YOUR MAJOR

Incoming freshmen usually approach their major in one of two ways: Either they self-consciously have absolutely no idea what they want to do, or they are dead set on pursuing a very specific path. There are few students who may have a vague interest in a few areas or who have faith that by jumping into college, they will find the path that's right for them (or at least there are few who are willing to admit it). But, as it turns out, that might just be the best approach of all.

Almost a third of students enrolled in bachelor's degree programs changed majors within three years of their initial enrollment, according to one study (Leu 2017). Perhaps that's because many schools offer an incredible variety of majors—for instance, the University of Washington offers 280 majors and concentrations within majors. Many schools also have majors in fields that incoming freshmen likely couldn't even imagine before taking a class in that domain. How would you know that you have a passion for puppetry before participating in the Puppet Arts Program at the University of Connecticut or that you can actualize your dreams of becoming a survivalist through Plymouth State University's Adventure Education major?

Most schools won't require you to declare your major until the second semester of your sophomore year (and you probably shouldn't before then), but here are some tips for getting an early start on thinking about your major.

Take general ed classes or classes that seem interesting first. If Julie hadn't decided to take the class "Social Movements" to fill her "Social Analysis" general education requirement, she probably never would've declared sociology as her major. She was actually dead set on majoring in women's studies (despite the *endless* jokes of "But why isn't there a men's studies?" in response to which she'd respond, "That's called history"). Then she took "Social Movements" and realized she was much better suited for sociology. But even if you don't have requirements to fill, don't be afraid to take a class in a discipline that seems a little offbeat or uncharacteristic. You just never know if you'll happen upon an area of study that you're surprisingly passionate about.

One of the best pieces of advice Anna was given before going into her freshman year was: "Don't marry your major." Much like dating different people before settling down, trying different areas of study helps you refine what you are looking for. It's okay to change majors, drop majors, and return to majors—it's all part of figuring out what you actually want to spend your college years (ahem, life) working on.

But beyond possibly encountering a new, awesome discipline, filling your general requirements just buys you some time to give your major some more thought. It allows you to get to know yourself better in other capacities—development that could easily lead to a better understanding of what you need and want to get out of your education.

Be honest with yourself. There's nothing wrong with knowing what you want and going after it. If you're sure you're destined to be a doctor, a philosopher, or a linguist, then go for it. But make sure to periodically check in with yourself and confirm that you enjoy what you're doing and the classes you're taking. It's important to pursue a path not because you think you should or because you always told yourself you would but because you're actually happy doing it and are getting something out of it. Especially if you're pre-professional (and especially if your parents pushed that track on you), just keep tabs on how you feel about your course of study. You should enjoy and feel inspired by your education, not feel obligated to pursue a certain course.

And just remember: The dirty secret about most majors—and most of a liberal arts education in general, for that matter—is that *very few* majors DIRECTLY translate to what you end up doing with your life. For example, consulting and finance firms frequently recruit humanities majors *because* of their more creative approach to problem-solving. Most anthropology majors don't end up doing extensive ethnographies for the rest of their lives, and many psychology majors hardly end up listening to and analyzing other people's problems (or at least they do on their own time in a thing called friendship). That's why it's so important to *enjoy* your major—it's more a structured way to enjoy the learning process and explore themes and concepts that fascinate you than it is professional training.

Also, keep an eye out for possible minors. A lot of students accidentally complete minors after taking multiple classes in an area of interest. If you feel like you're taking a lot of classes in an area technically outside of your major, check and see what that department's minor requirements are—you may have already completed them (or only need to take another class or two to do so, and at that point, why not?).

THE BOTTOM LINE: HOW TO BALANCE WORK AND LIFE

There are countless "self-help" books out there that claim to give you the key to happiness, the *secret to life*. These books pose some interesting theories about visualizing the reality you want, about changing yourself to create the ideal life—the suggestions go on and on. But if you ask Julie, there is no singular prescription for finding happiness. As a now 30-something, she's found only one key to happiness: Trying to have a life that balances work with everything else.

Finding this balance can be especially hard for women, though. Women have long been told we can have careers *and* families (*and* friendships, *and* hobbies, *and* the list goes on), and everything will just fall into place. The truth is, though, balancing the various parts of our lives is hard.

We certainly feel the strain of finding this balance while in school: We struggle to accommodate club meetings, rehearsals, and jobs with imminently due papers, seeing friends, and maybe going on a date or two, hopefully finding a couple of hours to sleep somewhere in there. After graduation, once we enter the "real" world rather than the insulated quasi-world of college campuses, and try to have careers instead of jobs and "serious" relationships instead of hook-ups, we are only faced with ratcheted-up, competing demands.

Unfortunately, there's no easy way to find the perfect balance for each of us; that "perfect" balance is dependent on and formed by each individual's unique struggles and goals. The hard truth is finding balance just takes time and experience—but actively practicing healthy ways of balancing our lives in college can do a lot to make the future balancing act that may dominate our adult lives a little more manageable. If we establish habits and routines that allow us to balance work (school) with our lives (friendships, relationships, and fun), we just might be able to carry them with us throughout our lives.

So how do we do this? It seems like we're often given self-evident, less-than-helpful advice like "just breathe" or "slow down!" So here are some platitude-free things college women can and should do to actually force some balance into their lives.

Schedule time devoted to your weakness. Maybe this is just the confluence of Julie's Type A personality and visual learning style, but she finds it incredibly helpful to take some time to plan out her week. Yes, this takes time, and yes, nearly all events are subject to change (largely due to everybody else's insane schedules), but having everything laid out before her somehow makes everything seem much more manageable: Her life is not just a swirling mass of commitments polluting her mind, popping up every time she's just about to fall asleep—it's all there, ready to be checked off.

It can also be particularly helpful to schedule time to attend to your weakness—to

ASK AN EXPERT

The Best Way to Approach Academics

My advice would be to take at least one class per semester in a subject you've never studied before. Go through the course catalog in detail, talk to older students about which professors or courses have blown their minds, and let yourself experiment! I'd also recommend trying out different schedules for the week in different semesters, such as playing around with morning vs. afternoon and evening classes. This is the first time most students will have such flexibility with their schedules, so it's a good time to try out which times of day are best for you (in terms of being in class vs. doing writing, reading, activities).

—Dr. Ellie Anderson, Pomona College

schedule balance into your life. If you're an incredibly social person, schedule time when you absolutely have to work. If you're incredibly driven and prone to getting caught up in school, schedule time when you have to take it easy and give your brain a break (hi, mindless chick-flick marathon) or (better yet) when you allow yourself to go out and be social.

In college, nobody reminds you to balance your life or tells you that too much work will drive you insane but that too little will defeat the point of being at college at all. Creating a schedule is one way to replace that governing influence and instill a bit more structure than just taking everything as it comes.

Take self-care seriously. Especially in an environment where everybody is doing their best impression of the Energizer Bunny—where they just keep going and going until they completely crash, without any kind of regularity or moderation—it can be hard to just stop for a second and take some well-deserved me-time. Every campus approaches academic pressure differently: At Columbia University, for instance, it's a cultural norm for most conversations to start with a somewhat competitive, weirdly braggy list of how much work each person has, whereas, at Stanford, the norm is to generally not appear to be working too hard or to be too stressed out despite an insane workload.

No matter your campus's cultural norm, you will probably feel stress and pressure to get your work done and do well on some level, but it's incredibly important to allow yourself to take time to take care of yourself—in a way that's distinct from having fun and partying. Your life in college shouldn't just be about working or having fun—studying hard and partying hard is hardly healthy.

Try to do something that feels therapeutic and restorative regularly. Whether it's taking a weekly yoga class or taking time on a weekend to bake something delicious (or actually cooking yourself a dinner that involves vegetables or some other nutritious component in some capacity)—whatever it is, it should be something that makes you feel taken care of, soothed, and whole. It should feel like the natural, active equivalent of taking medicine. It's the kind of stuff that is the first to be thrown off the to-do list in place of more concrete, externally dictated deadlines and events, but the kind of stuff that ultimately allows us to keep going, to meet those deadlines, and to be fully present at those events.

Cut yourself some slack. You worked hard to get into college. You studied for (most) of your high school exams, carefully compiled your college applications, and spent hours stressing out about impending deadlines (then possibly procrastinated, which caused you to stress out even more about how much you procrastinated). By your senior year of high school (right before the onset of Senioritis), you were probably thoroughly enmeshed in an ingrained cycle of hard work and stress—one that, though you know it's unhealthy, seems only natural to continue into college.

Here's the thing: You already got into college. That doesn't mean you can completely slack off. Even if you don't intend to go to graduate, medical, or law school (or if you don't *think* you intend to—you'd be surprised how many people change their minds about postgrad education), you *have* worked too hard to get into school (not to mention are spending too much time and money on it) to completely throw the experience away and slack off. It means you have to trust that you got into college because you know what you're doing. And building that trust can mean avoiding some common stress-inducing traps freshmen (and, unfortunately, sophomores, juniors, seniors, and even adults) fall into, including:

1. **Thinking that a single exam or grade in a single class will define the rest of your life:** It won't. Your life is more than a sum equation of what you did right and what you did wrong. It's far more complex (and messier, in the best possible way) than that. If you mess up, try to learn from it, view it as a growing experience, and move on.

2. **Considering every less-than-great grade as a personal failure:** You have to divorce grades and other quantifiable markers of "success" as wholly reflective of your personal worth. On the other hand, don't unilaterally blame your professors or TAs for your failures, either. Try to keep everything in perspective and remember that life isn't black and white, about being perfect or failing (and that "perfection" and "failure" can't be attributed to a single source). Embrace the gray. Use "failure" as a chance to learn about yourself and improve.

3. **Assuming that your friends, professors, or anybody else can sense when you're stressed or struggling and will or should automatically reach out to you:** Even people who know you well and love you are not mind readers. If you're struggling, seek help. Whether it's a matter of talking out a weird friendship situation with a parent or high school friend or finding a tutor to help you through a particularly rough class, the first move has to come from you. However, you'll find that once you do make that move, there are plenty of people and resources out there willing and able to support you.

At the end of the day, your academic experience at college is about *learning*—not about a number or letter on your transcript, not about cramming and memorizing. College is your time to find what drives you intellectually, what interests and excites you about the world, and how you want to interact with it (whereas high school was more about building academic skills and familiarity with the academic process).

Bottom line: You're not going to find your intellectual passion if you're more concerned with a score than with your personal comprehension and growth. So chill out about quantifying your academic competence. If you actually enjoy what you're learning and feel inspired by it, you're bound to succeed.

REFERENCE

Leu, Katherine. 2017. "Beginning College Students Who Change Their Majors Within 3 Years of Enrollment." Data Point. National Center for Education Statistics. December. https://nces.ed.gov/pubs2018/2018434/index.asp#.

CHAPTER 4

MIND, BODY, AND SPIRIT

How to Keep (All Parts of) Yourself Alive and Well

So here's a fun fact about being a real, live, autonomous human being: You are the only person in charge of keeping yourself alive. This sounds pretty basic. You've been alive for, what, around 18 years? Sure, your parents helped out with the whole avoiding mortality thing (especially those first few years)—we have to give credit where credit is due. But, come on, do we really need to talk about keeping ourselves healthy?

Yeah, we really do. As it turns out, when laced with the complete inundation of new experiences and stresses that are part and parcel of your freshman year, it's the most basic stuff—like your health and well-being—that tends to go out the window first in an effort to stay afloat. And that's a serious problem because if you don't feel well—in mind, body, and/or spirit—then you'll never be able to fully appreciate or perform well in any other part of your college experience.

Also, you'll face many *new* facets of well-being. From new eating (and drinking) habits to various new ways of experiencing

 DOI: 10.4324/9781003408932-4

and taking care of your body to tending to an overworked, constantly challenged mind, you're going to have a lot thrown at you. It turns out that really, truly taking care of yourself involves quite a bit more than flossing and begrudgingly eating your vegetables. Welcome to the adult world of health and wellness.

PHYSICAL HEALTH

When we hear the word "health," we tend to mentally zip to images of Instagram models who've mastered the "it girl" aesthetic, complete with morning routines full of cold showers and green powders that taste intolerable yet promise to turn you into Bella Hadid. While an immense amount of progress has been made (thank you, body positivity and neutrality movements), we are still constantly getting media cues that tell us our only options are to restrict and live an angelic life of supposed health or die a dramatic early death straight out of a cigarette ad. But being healthy doesn't have to be this polarized: There is definitely a happy medium we can (and should) strive for.

Beyond striking a balance, it's important to remember that physical health should be about how you feel, not how you look. This is often difficult for women to fully realize at any point in our lives (thanks, Facetune), but it often becomes a serious point of contention in college when our defenses are down due to the many other sources of stress and confusion, as well as the process of identity formation many of us go through. And it often strikes us in a few very specific ways.

THE MYTH OF THE FRESHMAN 15

There are a lot of crazy, scare-mongering myths floating around about the Freshman 15, but there is just one thing you need to know about it. Are you ready for this pearl of wisdom? Is your pen poised on paper, ready to capture this knowledge? Okay, here it is: The Freshman 15 is COMPLETE AND UTTER BULLSHIT.

To be fair, there is truth to the idea that your body may very well change your freshman year, but you're unlikely to gain 15 pounds. In fact, one study revealed that the average woman gains about four pounds in her freshman year (Beaudry et al. 2019).

But the whole "Freshman 15" thing is ridiculous beyond its basic factual inaccuracy. It's pretty unhealthy to compare your body to any kind of overarching norm or expectation. Instead, accept that you are at a physiological stage where your body can (and probably will) still change. Instead of freaking out about weight gain or loss, focus on feeling good in your body.

That being said, the reality is that freshman year is a time of serious life changes—and that undoubtedly extends to your eating and exercise habits. So, although our life view can generally be summed up as "Screw impossible beauty standards, love your body, and enjoy your life," there are also some nutrition-related changes you should be aware of from a perspective of health and practicality.

Beware of dining hall food. Despite many dining halls' attempts to offer vegan/gluten-free/low-fat/even-more-inedible-than-usual choices, most food exchanged for a meal card swipe is notoriously high in fat and calories and low on nutrition. We may be warned about this in terms of weight gain, but it's also important to consider the nutritional content of the food you consume in terms of your overall health.

For instance, Julie chalked up feeling tired *all of the time* her freshman year to her increased workload and happily sustained an impressive dedication to an all-carb diet. It wasn't until she was home for winter break and her mom made it her short-term life mission to constantly shovel vegetables into her like gas into a Hummer that she realized, *Oh, there's a REAL REASON why we should eat nutritious food—it HELPS US FUNCTION!* Which sounds ridiculously self-evident, but it's worth remembering, especially in the context of a culture that almost exclusively talks about food in terms of weight loss rather than health. It turns out eating well is not just about how you look but very much (and more importantly) about how you feel and how well you function.

A changed activity level. The thing about (supposedly) studying a lot and going to class is that you will not be required to move too much. This may seem great to those of us for whom moving is not our definition of a good time, but it's still necessary to at least attempt sometimes. Again, although we often talk about exercising in terms of weight loss (ugh, make it stop), it turns out exercise is actually really great for your physical and mental health. It's amazing how powerful endorphins are. There is nothing quite like the postexercise high, especially if you're feeling really worn down from studying and stress. It's counterintuitive, but when you feel really burned out from studying, going to the gym and running for even just 20 or 25 minutes can give you an empowering boost of energy.

Bottom line: Your campus probably has some form of a gym. Make an effort to get there regularly, or sign up for an exercise class that provides structure and external motivation to move your butt. Your weighted blanket will be there for you when you get back.

Newly available alcoholic beverages. Of course, college freshmen don't drink *ever* because *it's illegal.* But it's probably worth noting on a GENERAL LEVEL that a surprising number of freshmen don't seem to realize that alcoholic beverages have calories—an average serving of beer contains 153 calories, and a serving of vodka or tequila has 97 (National Institute on Alcohol Abuse and Alcoholism n.d.). That might not sound too bad, but few people successfully limit themselves to just one drink in a party setting, and many consume multiple drinks multiple times a week.

Besides calories, it's pretty well documented that alcohol causes plenty of long-term physical health risks over time—including high blood pressure, heart disease, cancer, and more—as well as mental health problems (Centers for Disease Control and Prevention 2022b). It's important to remember that everything is best *in moderation*.

Food = Comfort. We've said it before, and we'll say it again: The transition to college is really difficult for many women. Food can seem like an obvious way to find some comfort in an otherwise uncomfortable situation. Plenty of young women navigate the dining hall from an emotional perspective rather than from one of hunger or health. That's completely understandable, but the thing about emotional eating is that it's just not an effective way to deal with your feelings. It's a vicious cycle: You'll keep eating but never truly feel better because you're not dealing with the root of your feelings.

Basically, the ridiculous and repetitive "conversation" about women and the Freshman 15 (and eating and dieting in general, for that matter) is annoying and boring. We're constantly bombarded with strategies about how to eat to produce the "best" (i.e., thinnest) bodies. We say screw that. Here are the real things to remember about eating and nutrition:

◇ **Be gentle with yourself:** Try not to psyche yourself out about the Freshman 15. Accept that you may very well gain weight—and if you do, the world as you know it won't implode. Although media images try to encourage dieting away that extra layer of fat women naturally have for things like CHILDBIRTH, it's natural for us to have body shapes of all kinds. Focus on eating in a way that makes you feel healthy and whole, beyond a number on a scale or nutrition label.

It's also normal to feel like you want to make a health or lifestyle change, but it's important to understand that most eating disorders develop between the ages of 18 and 21 (Jacobson 2023), so if your thoughts around food ever start to get scary or intense (and we'll discuss that more soon), it's important to reach out for help.

◊ **Bodies change for many reasons:** We can all gain or lose weight for a number of reasons, including changes in our mental health, sleep patterns, or other underlying health problems (Dold et al. 2022). If your weight changes, instead of focusing on a number on a scale, it's worth checking in with yourself and trying to evaluate some of the deeper reasons why that may have happened.

◊ **It's okay to enjoy food:** It's really okay to enjoy your life, and that can often mean eating things that aren't necessarily "healthy" for you. Have that late-night piece of pizza with your friends. Have cake on your roommate's birthday. As long as you don't eat less-than-healthy food for every meal, every single day, in obscenely huge amounts, you'll be fine.

WHEN OUR BODY BECOMES THE ENEMY: NEGATIVE BODY IMAGE AND EATING DISORDERS

Although we accept that we'll be challenged intellectually and will face a new, adult reality in college, we are often unprepared for the way our bodies are included in the transition to this new reality: Our bodies are often the sites for this struggle and the receptacle of our frustration and exploration.

We've all been inundated with negative images and conceptions of unrealistic beauty standards practically since birth, and the struggle to compromise our normal human bodies with these impossible images hardly abates in college. Eating disorders, as well as a general disordered body image, run rampant among college-aged women. In fact, the National Eating Disorders Association estimates that between 10 and 20% of women in college suffer from an eating disorder (Jacobson 2023). And despite eating disorders often being stereotyped as an affluent White girl problem, women of color have about the same, or greater, lifetime prevalence of any eating disorder as White women (Nawaz and Lincoln Estes 2022). No matter their background, all college-age women are susceptible to falling into these traps.

But what is it about college specifically that can so strongly impact the way we view and treat our bodies?

Perfect girls, perfect students, perfect bodies. Female college students tend to be pretty competitive. They're used to constant pressure to be the best, to achieve as much as possible, to get into the school of their dreams—a pressure that permeates their entire existence.

One might think that getting into college would ease that burden and reduce the need for a coping mechanism like disordered eating. But there's not a switch that can turn off the pressure we've felt for years—especially for bright women constantly pushing themselves to be "better."

Eating disorders aren't always about food…or even your body. It's well documented that eating disorders aren't solely a response to feeling "fat"—they can function as coping mechanisms, especially in times of vulnerability and fear, two emotions that are in full supply when making the transition to college. Some young women view an eating disorder as a way to instill control in a world that seems to have completely shifted overnight: They feel that the only way to cope with an external environment seemingly beyond their control, with changing support networks and different routines, is to turn inward, to impose sanctions on their own body and derive power from the concrete effects they produce. In reality, they just lose more control as their disorder starts to dictate their feelings and actions.

But what can I actually DO? There are few sources of real, concrete advice for how to productively combat an eating disorder or negative body image. There's a valid reason for that: There are very few concrete things to be done in the face of a variety of intersecting and unfortunate social realities based on myriad causes, including centuries of ingrained sexism that ultimately cause these feelings and behaviors among women. The ultimate goal may be to end the destructive social forces at the core of these feelings, but pragmatically, that may take a while. In the meantime, here are a few productive tips to keep in mind that will hopefully help you or a friend consider this grossly sexist reality in a way that's much healthier and more productive for you.

If you feel you have a negative body image: *Realize that this is bigger than you.* Most of us understand that negative body image is a struggle for many women, but that understanding is more cerebral than it is something that productively allows us to manage and moderate our feelings. But here's the thing—being able to really deconstruct the way negative body image is deeply embedded in society and enforced by external sources does *so* much to moderate those feelings. Understanding that billion-dollar industries make a ton of money by making us feel bad about our bodies (so that they can then sell us crap to "fix" them) and that we have lived in the context of a society that sought to limit and oppress women in any way possible, including encouraging us to feel held back by our bodies for centuries, does so much to make this struggle feel less like a personal failure and more like an external roadblock.

Fake it until you make it. Externalizing the insecurities trapped in our heads can make them feel more tangible and manageable. If you actively practice externalizing self-acceptance and self-love, soon enough, it won't feel as forced. Self-love is at the root of any good relationship (with yourself, of course, but with others as well) and at the root of success. Actively practicing self-love is necessary to eventually achieving it, so regularly tell yourself you're beautiful (seriously). Also, focus on making mindful choices that are right for *you*. Remember, you have no idea what's going on in others' heads (but chances are it's a terrifying web of their own insecurities). You can only know what you think and what you need, so practice silencing the other voices and simply, clearly asking yourself what your needs are, AND then do your best to fulfill them.

Just say screw it. This is way easier said than done, but good lord, hating yourself is *exhausting.* Beyond being stupid and completely self-destructive and unhealthy, it just takes up SO MUCH TIME. It takes up so much space in your mind and emotional energy— energy you could expend on something that actually matters. You can't be digitally altered to perfection like so many of the influencers on our feeds. You are not a frat boy's ideal (nor would you ever want to be that pornified, two-dimensional version of a human). The sooner you accept and embrace the irrefutable reality of your individuality, the sooner you'll start really enjoying your life. Because here's the secret the beauty and weight loss industries don't want you to know: Physically changing whatever you're insecure about won't make you happy. The process of trying to change yourself will make you miserable, and you'll soon realize that life's difficulties still happen to conventionally attractive people. Focus on living *your* life.

If you feel you have an eating disorder: We are not experts on eating disorders, but luckily, there are plenty of experts and resources out there, such as:

◇ *The National Eating Disorders Association* (NEDA; www. nationaleatingdisorders.org): NEDA is dedicated to supporting individuals and families affected by eating disorders and serves as a catalyst for prevention, cures, and access to quality care.

◇ *Overeaters Anonymous* (OA; www.oa.org): OA uses a 12-step program to help individuals recover from compulsive eating.

◊ *Your campus's health center.* Chances are, your campus's health center also has eating disorder-related resources, such as a peer-support group or medical professionals knowledgeable about the topic and able to direct you to the help you need.

What if OTHER people have eating disorders or make you feel bad about your body? Did you ever have a moment (or many) in a high school cafeteria when a friend ("friend") looked at something delicious on your plate and passive aggressively said something like, "Wow, I wish I could eat like that," or "Are you sure you really want to eat that?" You're probably more than eager to leave behind those messed-up frenemy relationships in high school.

The thing is, these girls don't just disappear in college, and they're not always immediately identifiable. If you become close with a girl like this, you might eat with her frequently, which means regularly surrounding yourself with this destructive mentality. So what do you do if you (otherwise) like this girl but feel uncomfortable with these comments, and especially if you start to feel like they're getting to you on a deeper level?

◊ **Be transparent:** It can be hard, but be open and honest about your own struggles. Try to talk about how you worry about your body image (we all do to some extent) and especially how you work through it. Never underestimate how being transparent about *anything* you struggle with can be the best way to help others who may have felt like they were the *only* ones struggling with the same thing. Feeling less alone, like a problem isn't reflective of a personal failing, can be indescribably therapeutic and productive. Nip weird comments about food in the bud: Be upfront and tell your friend you feel those types of comments and mentality are destructive.

◊ **Remember, it's not about you:** Girls who make shaming comments about the way you eat don't think you're fat— they think *they're* fat. Beyond any reality about her or your body, girls who make these comments are ultimately deeply affected by a society that encourages women to feel insecure about themselves. Once you realize that feeling personally offended by her comments is futile, it'll take you to a mental space where you may meet her comments with compassion, which is what she really needs.

Julie personally knows what this struggle can feel like. In her freshman year, in an effort to appear as if she was thriving when she actually felt lost and helpless, she took her feelings of confusion and desperation out on her body. Although she had struggled with body image in high school, she always thought that somehow she would just outgrow it and any other personal struggles in college. However, she found the transition to college difficult, and her body took the biggest brunt of that adjustment; her body felt like the only controllable thing in a life of new chaos. Everybody around her, influenced by a society that equates weight loss with self-improvement, viewed her weight loss as a success, as an indication that she was doing well rather than an indicator that she was deeply struggling.

Over winter break, though, she realized that something needed to change. Especially in college, we women are so distracted by our bodies, by the shame and blame we feel on a daily basis, that we're less productive and feel less capable of advocating for ourselves. The very things we go to college to achieve—career success, ambitions, and leadership potential—are hampered due to the way we equate insecurities about our bodies with our sense of worth on all levels. We don't view ourselves as the subjects of our own lives but as objects. Although it's difficult, the change has to start now, in college, when we still have a shot at reclaiming our bodies and refusing to let the ways others view and want to control them hold us back from achieving all that we're capable of.

EMOTIONAL HEALTH

If you know anything about college, it's probably that it's supposed to be the best four years of your life. The truth is (as we've hopefully made abundantly clear by now) that college is a *really* big transition—one that isn't quite the carefree experience everybody makes it out to be. In fact, framing it that way produces a *lot* of social and psychological pressure that can often—somewhat counterintuitively—produce a lot of new emotions that are challenging to navigate. And, unfortunately, nobody is really honest enough about this before you're thrown into it. There are plenty of things that may trigger emotional challenges, including these specific triggers:

◇ **Stress:** This may be the most obvious mental strain on college students, but alas, it is the most universal and consistent. Students of *all* ages bump up against stress on a pretty continuous basis, and sadly, it seems that few ever really develop an effective strategy for dealing with it. Many (if not most) just accept it as a permanent aspect of life and let it slowly erode their well-being. Super healthy.

☛ *Solution*: Although you probably can't eliminate stress from your life, you can put effort into developing certain skills that can make a world of difference in terms of how you interact with it. Time management is essential: Try scheduling out everything you have to do so it feels more manageable. Force yourself to carve out time devoted to self-care—to doing something just for *you*. Get to know your own work patterns, and don't give in to the social construct of stress culture (what others do or *claim* to do to get their work done). Focus on what *you* need to do to get *your* work done. Also, refer to Chapter 3 on academics for more tips on how to manage stress and balance your life.

◇ **Social pressure:** So many rising freshmen are under the impression that they'll show up at school and good time after good time will fall into their lap. The truth is (as we will discuss further in Chapter 6), there's an art to having a healthy and well-rounded social life in college, and yet there remains this overarching ideal of college socializing that generates a weird pressure to have a ton of friends, to party all of the time, and to *document* that fun. Social media has a uniquely deleterious effect on *everybody's* social life (no matter what they say). At some point or another, we've all scrolled through Instagram and felt like everybody else was having so much more fun than us. We're constantly convinced that there's something great going on somewhere without us, which is stressful in its own way.

- ☛ *Solution*: Remember that this social pressure REALLY IS universal, no matter how anybody else comes off or how social she claims to be. Nobody can have a super awesome time always. Just try to focus on doing things that *you* think are fun and surrounding yourself with people who share those interests. Seriously, if partying isn't your thing, you're not going to have a good time with people who want to go out every night. On some level, you have to ask yourself *why* you feel like you need to go along with social conventions that don't interest you or aren't fun for you. Also, don't be afraid to say no. There is no reason to try to be everywhere at once, and at some point, it'll stop being fun and will just seem like another series of obligatory commitments. Life (and the college experience itself) is way too short to engage in things you think you're *supposed* to. Do what you *want* to do and screw the rest. You'll be a lot happier for it.

◇ **Constant change:** One aspect of college that students are usually unaware of before they are thrown into the thick of things is that you have to deal with change *constantly*. It comes in all forms: from the more concrete—classes change every semester, and you'll likely switch where you live every year—to the intangible—a high turnover in hook-ups, relationships, and even friendships. It's really easy to feel like the ground beneath your feet is anything but solid. Everybody around you is trying to figure out who they are, emotionally, intellectually, etc., and so are you. It's a process that necessitates adjustment and experimentation, which can mean that people and certain experiences may virtually disappear from your life relatively soon after they enter it. It's *a lot* to manage, especially if you don't deal well with change anyway.

☛ *Solution*: This one's a little more difficult to get a handle on. Change is just difficult and can lead to some messy emotions and heartbreak, especially in terms of friendships and relationships. The most salient tip we can give is to first try to develop a solid relationship with yourself. If you work intently on figuring out and knowing on a deeper level who you are, it'll be easier to handle and accommodate the changes swirling around you. Easier said than done, but you have to start somewhere, right? Also, being *aware* that this constant change is a pretty standard part of the college experience helps: *Everybody* feels like they've been swept up into a weird hurricane of constant transition. Once you realize it's not personal, it usually becomes easier to handle.

But beyond these specific triggers, the bottom line is college is just, well, A LOT. It's super easy to feel overwhelmed for no specific reason at all. If you start to feel like the world is closing in on you (or some lesser degree of that extreme), here are our top tips for keeping your feet on solid ground:

◊ **Take care of your physical health:** Refer to all of the prior nutrition tips because, as we already mentioned, eating well, exercising, and sleeping are all *incredibly important*, not just for trying to prevent your body from becoming a decrepit shell of your comparatively robust high school self but also for ensuring your emotional well-being. Also, drink a ton of water. Most of us are walking around dehydrated and wondering why we feel crappy. Drink water! It's SO EASY, and you'll feel SO GREAT! You're welcome in advance.

◊ **Designate time every day for YOU time:** College students often divide their time into working or socializing and almost accidentally omit designating time to one of the most restorative things they can do: having some alone time. Seriously, every day, do something that is just for you, something that makes you feel whole and personally taken care of. Whether it's baking yourself some cookies, going for a run, or reading a non-school book—whatever. Just take time to take care of yourself.

◊ **Learn who you are:** This is incredibly broad, but the bottom line is that if you know what you want, if you know what truly makes you happy and do your best to ignore what others think of you and whether or not others are judging you based on your decisions, then you will feel so much better on *every* plane of your existence. We promise you that.

DEPRESSION

Many college freshmen are disappointed to find that on a day-to-day basis, being an undergrad isn't necessarily the manically ecstatic experience society and the media are committed to insisting it is. There are as many happy and joyous occasions (hooking up without worrying about your younger sibling walking in on you, Taco Tuesday in the dining hall) as there are stressful and even disconcerting moments (your first major exam, feeling like you'll never find another best friend).

For many students, these experiences even out into a feeling of basic contentment, but others may develop some persistent feelings of sadness and/or anxiety. Maybe it's a feeling you've had before that seems newly augmented and somewhat uncontrollable, or maybe it's a completely novel (and thus pretty scary) experience. Either way, it's possible that these aren't just isolated feelings but depression.

Although there doesn't seem to be a ton of transparency about it, feeling depressed is actually a pretty common experience among college-aged students. In fact, a recent study found that one in three

The Truth About Depression

Many people buy into the myth that a person can only be depressed when life isn't going well. They may come to college and love it and therefore don't understand why they are depressed or even beat themselves up about feeling this way or not get help. But it is so important to get treatment as soon as you notice a problem. The sooner you tackle *any* problem, the better the outcome, and things snowball fast once you are in the throes of depression. You may stop doing homework, then get bad grades from which you can't bounce back. You might sleep through classes and appointments or fail to respond to friends, who might then get mad at you.

The first place to go for help is the school counseling center, usually located in the department of student affairs. Most colleges offer free counseling to students as part of their tuition, and there is no problem too big or too small for counseling. If they can't offer the help you need, they will refer you to someone in the community who can.

—Kathryn Stamoulis, PhD, LMHC, Educational Psychologist

college students experiences significant depression and anxiety (Bowe 2023). Women are also twice as likely to suffer from depression as men (Brody, Pratt, and Hughes 2018). There is no single understanding of depression—its myriad causes and symptoms vary depending on the individual who experiences them—but here are some common symptoms, according to the National Institute of Mental Health (2023):

◊ persistent sad, anxious, or "empty" mood;
◊ feelings of hopelessness or pessimism;
◊ loss of interest or pleasure in hobbies and activities;
◊ decreased energy, fatigue, or feeling slowed down;
◊ difficult sleeping or oversleeping; and
◊ changes in appetite or unplanned weight changes.

Although depression is a medical condition that can be genetic in origin, your environment also impacts your risk for depression, including stresses that are especially relevant to college students, like living away from family for the first time, feeling overwhelmed by a complete change in routine and lifestyle, feeling alone, worrying about finances, and feeling stress generally.

So what should you do if you feel this way? First and foremost, talk to somebody about it. It's hard to believe there are people who can actually help you when you feel overwhelmingly depressed and hopeless, but there really are. Chances are, your campus has resources specifically designed to help depressed students, and you can also dial 988, the National Suicide Prevention Lifeline.

If you notice that a friend is exhibiting symptoms of depression, the key thing to remember is that you should in no way ignore or enable those symptoms. If you truly think your friend is struggling with depression, don't make excuses for why she missed obligations or encourage her to do things that'll interfere with her mental health (like drinking). If you are truly concerned about her, you should first try to talk to her about it. Let her know that there are absolutely things she can do to help her feel better, and she needs to reach out to a professional. If she rebuffs you or refuses to get help, it's really important to try to keep talking to her or, eventually, get her the help she needs but won't get. Many people feel like they're going behind their friend's back by doing so, but in reality, you could be saving her life.

Basically, remember that—like most of the struggles you may experience in college—depression is not a personal failing or your individual downfall. It's something that happens to so many college students, and there are real, effective ways to get help. There is no shame in reaching out to any of the aforementioned resources or even a trusted friend or family member—in fact, it may just be the best thing you can do for yourself.

Mental Health

I struggled so much with my mental and physical health during my freshman year. The first thing to remember is that even if your support system is back home and your friends are now scattered across the country, that is still a system you can and should count on. Further, when you first move to school, focus on fostering daily routines that you can rely on—it will provide a sense of familiarity and comfort in a new environment.

One of the things that helped me most was being out in nature and trying to express myself creatively. During my freshman year, I would sit in the park and read and write, which was a very calming and meditative process that helped me a lot. When I was stuck back in my dorm, I focused my energy on writing music and little art projects. It helped me to express the intense emotions I was feeling in a positive and fulfilling way.

—Grace, Columbia College Chicago

SEXUAL HEALTH

Let's be honest: One of the strongest associations people have with college is sexual freedom. So many people think of college as an extended free-for-all orgy, a string of hook-ups, a monogamy-free island of deviance. We (predictably) have a few thoughts on this.

First, college isn't exactly a cesspool of casual, carefree, never-ending sex. Statistics show that *most* college students aren't hooking up with the type of frequency the outside world thinks they are, if they're hooking up at *all* (which, again, many are not). Even among those who do regularly hook up (however you choose to define that expressly ambiguous term), there are still plenty of students out there who prefer (and successfully have) long-term relationships, and even those who are perfectly happy remaining abstinent (even if temporarily) and everything in between. There's hardly a single sexual profile that can be applied to all college students.

Secondly, most people would be surprised by what many freshmen *don't* know about sex (big shout out to abstinence-only sex education on this one!). Freshmen enter college with a huge range of sexual experience, knowledge, and cultural messaging that undoubtedly shapes their experiences at school and determines with whom, how, and how often they hook up. So, again, there's no single sexual profile of the average college student.

Finally—and this is specifically where this section of this chapter comes in—there's a lot of sexual health-related information women *need* to know before they enter college. Some topics are fun to talk about (enthusiastic consent, masturbation, etc.), and some are really difficult (the upsetting prevalence of abusive relationships and sexual assault on all college campuses across this country, for instance). But it's important that we cover the good *and* the bad: Knowledge is power, and the more you know about sex—in terms of your own sexual health and the sex-related obstacles you might encounter—the better you'll be able to make choices and design experiences that are right for you.

THE GOOD: TAKING CONTROL OF YOUR SEXUAL HEALTH

Nothing would make us happier than having the ability to sit you all down and take you through some basic comprehensive sex ed. We'd laugh, we'd cringe, we'd awkwardly start eating a banana intended for…other purposes. It would be A HOOT AND A HALF. Unfortunately, we don't have the time or space to do that (although, luckily, a bunch of far more competent people did and do—check out the resources included in this section for more information). But here are some sexual health basics to get you started.

The Basics

So, for the people who grew up in cultural environments that shamed them for the basic fact that they are humans with sexual organs that can be used for purposes other than reproduction (BLASPHEMY), here's the deal: Sex can describe a range of behaviors and activities. The heterosexist understanding of sex involves penis-in-vagina intercourse (which the cool kids call "P-in-V"), but plenty of people engage in other types of intercourse (like anal or oral), touching (oral, genital, or anal), and beyond. Basically, how one defines and engages in sex is up to an individual and their partner (and, in our humble opinion, shouldn't be defined or sanctified by anybody else).

It's also worth noting that some people have higher sex drives than others. We undeniably live in a hypersexualized culture. We're surrounded by sexualized images (especially of women, and really especially of demeaned and objectified women, but that's a whole other rant). But it's totally normal to have varying levels of sexual desire—as an individual or at specific times in your life (or even in your menstrual cycle). Basically, we're all indoctrinated to believe that any sexual desires we have or behaviors we engage in that deviate from the very heterosexist norm that's shoved down our throats in popular culture is WRONG and that we're BAD, but that's bullshit—sex is a complex and individual thing. So, on a basic level, don't worry so much about *what* you want to do: Just be cautious and smart about *how* you're doing it.

Staying Safe

Many of us can recall being halfway out the door on our way to meet our friends and hearing our mother's semi-panicked voice yelling after us: "MAKE GOOD CHOICES!" You probably rolled your eyes then, but she had a point: It's vitally important to make choices based on some solid knowledge. And the first critically important decision you should make about sex—if you choose to have it—is how you're going to protect yourself.

To clear up a common misconception right off the bat, using birth control is not just about preventing pregnancy but also about protecting yourself against STIs (sexually transmitted infections; see the sidebar on this topic). Therefore, even if you don't have sex with men or don't have P-in-V intercourse and conclude you probably won't get pregnant anytime soon, you should still be using some form of protection for health reasons.

So, without further ado, here's some information about the most popular forms of birth control and STI protection:

◊ Condoms:
   ☛ *Pros*: They're 98% effective with perfect use and 87% effective with typical use, widely available, and pretty easy to use (if we could figure out a way to demonstrate how to use them in print, we totally would, but alas, you'll have to follow the instructions yourself). Also, many college health centers give them out for FREE.
   ☛ *Cons*: They can break or slip off, rendering them ineffective. They also need to be used for *all* genital contact to effectively prevent pregnancy and/or STIs (which a lot of people don't realize).

◊ Oral contraceptives ("the pill"):
   ☛ *Pros*: It's a pill, so it's easy and painless to use, and it's proven to be pretty safe. It's also 99.7% effective with perfect use and 93% effective with typical use. It also can

have some awesome benefits, like clearing up mild acne and decreasing PMS symptoms. However, the pill does *not* protect against STIs, so you have to use condoms, too. There are also quite a few different types of the pill, and you should consult with your primary care doctor or gynecologist about which is right for you.

- ☛ *Cons*: You're supposed to take the pill at the same time every day, which can be challenging for busy college students. The pill can also have side effects for some, including (somewhat ironically) decreased sexual desire, weight gain, and/or increased depression and/or anxiety.

◇ Intrauterine devices:
- ☛ *Pros*: If you feel that you're going to be sexually active for the next few years of your life and don't plan on getting pregnant during that time, getting an IUD is a great way to go. IUDs are small devices inserted into your uterus by a sexual healthcare provider and remain there for a number of years. There are two types of IUDs: hormonal, which release the hormone levonorgestrel and last for around five years, and nonhormonal, which are made of copper and can stay in place for at least ten years. Both interfere with sperm mobility and egg fertilization to prevent pregnancy and are 99+% effective with perfect *and* typical use.
- ☛ *Cons*: The biggest con associated with IUDs is that, like the pill, they *don't prevent STIs*. You have to use them with a condom to prevent disease transmission. Also, if there are any complications at any time during the IUD's residency in your uterus, you will need access to an adequate healthcare provider who can help out. There can also be a relatively high cost of insertion.

Sidenote about birth control. If you're sexually active and use a method that is applied immediately before sex, you should carry it around with you at all times just in case—and carry them in a hard case and for a relatively limited amount of time so they aren't damaged or degraded. Many girls are afraid this will make them look "slutty," but seriously, screw that. Anybody who thinks that is a slut-shaming jerk and isn't worth your time. Safety first, always.

These are just a few of your options. There are plenty of other methods of birth control (like the patch, the shot, hormonal implants, spermicide, and more), and if none of the above methods seem right for you, make sure to check out websites like Scarleteen and Bedsider. Both have amazing, comprehensive descriptions and

WHAT IS PLAN B?
HINT: IT'S NOT THE ABORTION PILL

Plan B tends to get a bad rap in the media, and there seems to be a lot of confusion about what it is. Here are the facts:

♦ **WHO should use it:** Anybody whose birth control failed or who didn't use it during sex and wants to avoid pregnancy.

♦ **WHAT it is:** Emergency contraception, which is not equivalent to an abortion, is made from a one-time dose of a higher level of hormone your body makes naturally.

♦ **HOW it works:** These pills contain a hormone called *levonorgestrel*, which prevents pregnancy by delaying ovulation (the egg and sperm never meet up). Therefore, to reiterate, it has no effect on an established pregnancy and is ineffective if a woman has already ovulated. You must take the actual pill within 72 hours after unprotected sex and can get it from a drugstore or possibly your college's health center without a prescription or ID.

♦ **WHEN you should feel ashamed about using it:** NEVER. Look, there are wildly misguided people out there who have (generally ignorant) opinions about things like Plan B and might try to make you feel bad about using it. But it's *your* life, and plenty of women fought for your right to make these types of decisions so that you *can* have the life you want. Take advantage of it and know you did the best thing for you.

tools to help you decide what form of birth control is right for you. You can (and probably should) also visit your health center or, better yet, a gynecologist for solid advice and resources.

But although having the technical aspects of safe sex down is super important, there are some more nuanced things to remember about having safe sex generally. Here are your essential keys to safe sex:

◊ If you're having sex with dudes:
  ☛ You should be using two methods of birth control at any given time: ideally, condoms for protection against STIs, as well as another method with a high effectiveness for pregnancy prevention, such as hormonal methods like the pill or IUD.
  ☛ You really shouldn't use methods like the "pull out"/"pull and pray"/"withdrawal method," which is only 78% effective with typical use. Although it's *possible* for this method to be effective, it only is if the male partner has some exceptional self-control and, ideally, if you're tracking your menstrual cycle and taking your waking temperature daily to find out exactly when you're ovulating. Let's face it: Neither is exactly characteristic of college students.

◊ If you're having sex with anybody:
  ☛ We have to mention that abstaining from sex is the only 100% fail-proof method for not getting pregnant or STIs. It's totally realistic for some and completely unrealistic for others. If you know that it's unrealistic for you, be honest with yourself and figure out the best way to regularly protect yourself.
  ☛ If you're sexually active, get tested for STIs regularly. Even if you're super careful and safe, you owe it to yourself and your partner(s) to be 100% sure about your sexual health. Many college health centers provide testing, as do Planned Parenthood centers and other health centers across the country.

THE TRUTH ABOUT STIS

The traditional sex ed approach to STIs seems to be to break out a bunch of terrifying, close-up clinical photos of sexually transmitted infections that will force you to wake up sobbing when they randomly appear in an otherwise satisfying dream. Yet even viewing such graphic pictures is ultimately a meager source of competition for the formidable force of nature that is adolescent hormones—and statistics prove just that. In fact, one in two sexually active persons will contract an STD/STI by age 25 (Planned Parenthood n.d.). So, instead, here's a straight rundown of three of the most common STIs. Hopefully, you'll get the picture and be smart enough to try to avoid them by using condoms.

HPV

HPV is the most common sexually transmitted infection: Nearly all sexually active people will get HPV at some point if they don't get vaccinated (Centers for Disease Control and Prevention 2022a). It can cause genital warts or small bumps that appear within weeks or months after being infected. There are more than 40 types of HPV, some of which can cause cancers like cervical cancer if left untreated. However, there are treatments, like freezing warts, topical medicines, and an HPV vaccine.

HERPES

Herpes is a viral infection of the genitals (Herpes 2) and/or mouth and lips (Herpes 1) transmitted through any type of sex as well as skin-to-skin contact. About one in six people between the ages of 14 and 49 have genital herpes, and most people don't have any symptoms other than sores, which occur during outbreaks (Johns Hopkins Medicine 2020). Medications exist to help treat symptoms and reduce the frequency of outbreaks, but there is no cure.

CHLAMYDIA

Chlamydia is a genital, anal, or throat bacterial infection, and an estimated 1 in 20 sexually active young women between the ages of 14 and 24 have it (Centers for Disease Control and Prevention 2023b). There are often no symptoms, but symptoms can involve yellow-green vaginal discharge, bleeding between periods, and/or burning during urination (lovely, right?). Chlamydia can be treated with oral antibiotics, but the disease increases the risk for other infections like pelvic inflammatory disease (which can cause infertility).

☛ You should always be in charge of your own sexual health. As distrustful as it sounds, never rely on your partner to provide protection. You owe it to yourself to not allow any element of chance to enter the picture.

SEXUAL HEALTH RESOURCES

To learn more about how to sexually empower and care for yourself, check out these resources. Also, consider making an appointment with a gynecologist or visiting a Planned Parenthood or other women's health care center before you leave for college. After all, they're the real professionals.

♦ **Bedsider** (http://bedsider.org): Bedsider is your one-stop shop for in-depth information about birth control. It offers a "method explorer" tool that allows you to explore and compare every type of birth control—from the perspectives of "most effective," "party ready," "STI prevention," "easy to hide," and "do me now"—and addresses any questions you may have about each method. It also directs you to places where you can get each method and also has an array of fun and informative articles.

♦ **Scarleteen** (http://scarleteen.com): Scarleteen, which has been offering young adults advice about sex, sexual health, sexuality, and relationships since 1998, covers every one of these topics in a thoughtful, honest, and comprehensive way. If you've ever had any (and I do mean *any*) questions about sex, your body, and beyond, Scarleteen is the website to check out.

♦ **Planned Parenthood** (www.plannedparenthood.org): Planned Parenthood is the old standby and a godsend to millions of women. Its website offers a ton of incredibly useful information about sexual health—ranging from information about abortion, birth control, relationships, sex and sexuality, STIs, women's health, and beyond. They are probably best known for their physical centers, which offer an amazing array of general health services that are actually affordable for all women.

Sexual Empowerment

Okay, "sexual empowerment" might not be included in most comprehensive sex education programs, but it *should be*. Basically, women have been subjected to oppressive cultural forces that have sought to control our bodies and reproductive rights, as well as our sexual autonomy, for literally centuries. When the birth control pill was approved for contraceptive use in 1960 (although, incredibly, not available for *unmarried* women until 1972), it quite literally transformed women's lives. Women gained the unprecedented ability to control their reproductive systems and *plan* pregnancies, therefore delaying marriage and enabling them to make *autonomous decisions*. We've come a long way since that point (and arguably because of it), but unfortunately, the restrictive, shaming culture that dictates women remain "pure" and "chaste" that existed for centuries before the pill and the sexual revolution is still ingrained in our society.

It's these archaic ideas about women's sexuality that tend to make true sexual empowerment difficult. They're the forces that allow bullshit double standards about women and sex to persist. For example, college women frequently encounter the "slut/whore" dichotomy that simultaneously pressures women to be always sexually appealing and available yet also dictates that if they sleep around *too* much ("too much" being a pretty arbitrary amount), then they're sluts. Under the power of this double standard, women are considered weird if they're not sexually active enough (and are "virgin shamed") but considered whores if they're *too* sexually active (and are "slut shamed"). Women can't win under this ridiculous dichotomy of women's sexuality, which has nothing to do with our own pleasure or satisfaction and everything to do with limiting and oppressing us.

To destroy this double standard, women need to be vigilant about speaking out against it when they see evidence of it— when a guy *or* girl calls another girl a "slut" or "whore" based on the way she expresses her sexuality, when somebody pressures a girl to be sexually active when she has chosen to be abstinent, etc. But although that societal shift may take time, on a personal level, you can try to overcome that double standard by acknowledging that everybody has different levels of sexual experiences, comfort, and ways of expressing their sexuality—and that it's *all* good.

But even beyond the ideological shift that needs to happen, there are a few things you can actually *do* to claim your sexual empowerment, like masturbation. There's this weirdly pervasive myth out there that only guys masturbate. There are also some ridiculously archaic myths that masturbation is THE DEVIL'S WORK and can make you blind or crazy or damage your genitals. Oh, the ignorance! The truth is that women can and do masturbate as well—and for plenty of good reasons, like:

1. **It's healthy:** Masturbation releases stress and physical tension. Orgasms can act as a natural painkiller, and many women masturbate to ease menstrual cramps and/or back pain (Cleveland Clinic 2022).

2. **It's an awesome way to exercise your sexual autonomy and exploration:** Want to have an orgasm without worrying about STIs or pregnancy? Hi, masturbation. One study also showed that women who masturbate have higher self-esteem than those who don't (Cleveland Clinic 2022). It makes sense: Masturbating is literally the physical act of loving yourself, a basic concept women should wholeheartedly embrace in every aspect of their lives. Masturbating can enable you to take control of your sexuality in a really satisfying and beneficial way.

3. **Bettering sex with others:** Masturbating allows you to really get to know your body—what turns you on, what feels good. Instead of putting all the pressure on your partner to please you, knowing your body allows you to

take control. If you know what you like, you'll be able to communicate it to your partner and have awesome sex. Win–win.

Contrary to dominant depictions of college campuses as totally enlightened environments, sexism and close-mindedness related to sex and sexuality persist and can feed into some really ugly realities of sexual violence (which we'll discuss shortly). It's still *more* than possible, though, to claim your sexuality in college. Part of the college experience is figuring out who you are, what you want and need, and feeling empowered to go after it, and that certainly relates to your body and sexuality as much as it does your mind.

YOUR OTHER SYLLABUS
SEXUAL EMPOWERMENT

Yes Means Yes!: This volume of 27 essays (edited by Jaclyn Friedman and Jessica Valenti) promotes a genuine understanding of and respect for female sexual pleasure by reframing the common "No Means No" anti-rape campaign—the general negative approach to women's sexuality—by positing that instead we should celebrate women's sexual autonomy.

What You Really, Really Want: Jaclyn Friedman's awesome book on female sexual empowerment essentially answers the question: "Given all the conflicting messages young women get about their sexuality, how do they figure out what they—you guessed it—really, really want?" This book is an absolute *must-read* for any woman who wants to really explore and own her sexuality (so, all of us).

The Purity Myth: Valenti takes on the U.S.'s cultural tendency to place women's worth entirely on their sexuality and argues that women should be valued less for their sexuality (or purity) and more for values like honesty, kindness, and altruism.

THE BAD AND UGLY: ABUSIVE RELATIONSHIPS AND SEXUAL ASSAULT

It's repulsive how little information incoming freshmen are presented with in terms of the nastier things they might encounter regarding sex and sexual relationships. Maybe it's because colleges want to cover up incidents of sexual assault that make them look bad (as so many do) or because they think it's "inappropriate" to get into topics that are difficult to address. The fact remains, though, that while abusive relationships and sexual assault are by no means a college-specific phenomenon, they *do* happen at colleges across the country—at alarming rates, no less. There are plenty of other issues we could get into here (and we will certainly direct you to other resources that address those issues), but two (unfortunately) incredibly prevalent issues that we'll address here are abusive relationships and sexual assault.

ABUSIVE RELATIONSHIPS

Here are the facts:
◇ People between the ages of 18 and 24 are the most at-risk age group for experiencing intimate partner violence (NVRDC 2020).
◇ One survey found that 10.1% of students who had been in a relationship since entering college experienced intimate partner violence (NVRDC 2020).
◇ People between the ages of 18 and 24 experience the highest rates of stalking among adults, and the most common stalkers are former intimate partners (Stalking Prevention, Awareness, and Resource Center n.d.).

What Is an Abusive Relationship?

Any pattern of behavior used to gain or maintain power and control over a partner is considered abusive (Love Is Respect 2020). It can include:

◇ physical abuse (intentional, unwanted contact with you);

◇ emotional and verbal abuse (threats, insults, intimidation, isolation);

◇ sexual abuse (any behavior that coerces someone to do something sexually they don't want to do);

◇ digital abuse (reading your text messages, bullying, or harassing via social media); and

◇ stalking (when someone watches, follows, or harasses you repeatedly, making you feel unsafe).

Abusive relationships aren't relegated to a certain population or type of couple—they don't distinguish between race, religion, age, sexual orientation, etc. They can affect anyone and take the form of a *pattern* (if it happens once, chances are it's not an isolated incident and will happen again), as well as a *cycle* of power and control that looks something like Figure 4.2.

There is no designated starting point for this cycle, and one can be in an abusive relationship without meeting every single point mentioned, but each category generally includes the tactics of abuse shown in Figure 4.3.

Being a Bystander

Although many people think abuse is a "private" matter restricted to just the two people in an abusive relationship, the truth is that abusive relationships can impact (at least) three people (and usually more): the abuser, the target, and the bystander. Although

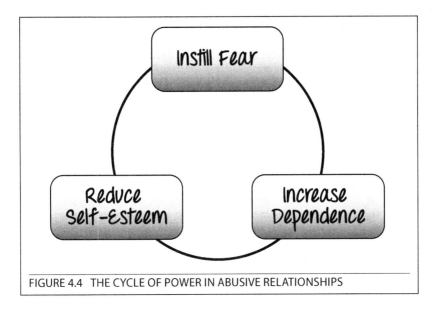

FIGURE 4.4   THE CYCLE OF POWER IN ABUSIVE RELATIONSHIPS

abuse isn't always obvious to outsiders, there are plenty of instances where people will witness somebody physically, verbally, or sexually abusing someone else and do absolutely nothing about it. In fact, people are often *less* likely to interfere if they feel the two people involved in a confrontation know each other and are in a relationship. Despite having the power to help—despite the fact that they may be the victim's *only* chance for help—most people won't do anything.

Why? Bystanders often feel it "isn't their place" to intervene or won't do so because they're worried it will be a difficult and uncomfortable situation for *them*. Yes, inserting yourself into a situation that doesn't directly involve you can be challenging, and you shouldn't do so if you feel you could be putting yourself in danger. But if there's a chance you can prevent or intervene in domestic abuse and possibly provide the help somebody desperately needs, you should take it.

Instill Fear

- **Threats and Rumors:** The abuser may threaten to harm him- or herself, others, or the target as a means of controlling him or her. The abuser may threaten to kill him- or herself, expose secrets, spread rumors about, or send/post inappropriate pictures of the target to others should he or she try to leave or get help.
- **Intimidation and Physical Violence:** The abuser may physically assault his or her target, throw things at him or her, or intimidate him or her by driving recklessly or shouting.
- **Stalking:** About 3.4 million people over the age of 18 are stalked each year in the U.S. and 30% of stalking victims are stalked by a current or former intimate partner (U.S. Department of Justice, 2009). Constant texting/calling/e-mailing when partners are apart, insisting to accompany a partner everywhere, or showing up uninvited all qualify as stalking, especially if the behavior continues after a relationship ends. Although abusers may claim to be "looking out for" their current/former partner, they are in fact violating their partner's privacy and attempting to control them.

Increase Dependence

- **Violation of Personal Space:** The abuser may engage in unwanted physical contact or violate virtual privacy by hacking into e-mail or social media accounts.
- **Isolation:** The abuser prohibits his or her partner from seeing or spending time with anybody outside the relationship—especially those the abuser may feel intimidated by (such as another potential partner). A common defense is that "Jealousy is a sign of love," but in this case it's actually a sign of abuse.
- **Testing:** The abuser constantly tries to "test" how much the target loves him or her, such as limiting free time only to spending time together and engaging in undesired sexual acts. Abusers who test their targets often use phrases like "If you loved me, you would . . ." and sometimes create alternate online profiles to test their target's online activity (and fidelity).

Reduce Self-esteem

- **Limiting Self-Expression:** Because of their abuser's controlling behavior, targets of abusive relationships are limited by their inability to join clubs or other groups, having their free time dictated or limited, being told how they should dress or how much make up they should wear (especially being slut-shamed for their choices), and even what types of birth control they should (or shouldn't) use. Essentially, the abused are asked to give up what they want and need in the name of what their abusers want.
- **Emotional Abuse:** Emotional abuse includes putting down somebody (i.e., telling a partner that they dress like a slut, are overweight and/or stupid, etc.) and making him or her feel guilty for what his or her abuser sees as faults, which reflect poorly on the abuser. On the other hand, abusers will often make grandiose and manipulative statements like, "You are the only person for me" or "I can never love anyone the way I love you"—used to make the abused person feel emotionally connected to the abuser.

FIGURE 4.5

So, how can you be more than a bystander? The Ending Violence Association of British Columbia has some ideas ("Be More than a Bystander" n.d.):

◊ If you don't know the target:

☛ The most obvious step is to refuse to *participate* in or encourage any kind of abusive behavior. If you see that somebody else is being targeted, stand near them so that the person causing harm knows they are being monitored.

☛ You can directly ask the person you suspect is the target of abuse if they are okay or if there's any way you can help. However, it's safer to vocally address the person causing harm by telling them to stop and warning them that you will call the police if they don't.

◊ If the target is a friend:

☛ Talk to your friend. Tell them you are concerned and want to help. Emphasize that it's not their fault, that they don't deserve such treatment, and that they aren't alone. Avoid any judgment, and don't confront your friend during an episode of violence, as you could be putting yourself in a dangerous position as well.

☛ Ask them if they would like help developing a plan or finding resources that could help (like the ones listed below). If you are discussing options for reporting and/or support, offer to go with them to the police, campus counselor, or health center. Accessing resources and reporting should always be the choice of the target or person experiencing harm. For a more detailed plan, visit the National Coalition Against Domestic Violence website (http://ncadv.org).

☛ Recognize your limitations. The cycle of violence can be physically, emotionally, and psychologically intense. There may be instances where you perceive that your

HOW YOU CAN GET HELP

Resources for Abusive Relationships

These organizations and websites can offer you far more information and direct plans for action. If you or somebody you know is in an abusive relationship, don't hesitate to check in with these resources as soon as you can.

- ◆ **Love Is Respect** (http://loveisrespect.org): Love Is Respect is a project of the National Domestic Violence Hotline that aims to disrupt and prevent unhealthy relationships and intimate partner violence by empowering young people through inclusive and equitable education, support, and resources. You can also access the National Dating Abuse Hotline by calling 1-866-331-9474, using the live chat feature on their website, or texting "LOVEIS" to 22522.
- ◆ **National Network to End Domestic Violence** (NNEDV; www.nnedv.org): NNEDV is an organization dedicated to creating a social, political, and economic environment in which violence against women no longer exists.

friend is in an abusive relationship but feel their choices of seeking help are limited. You can encourage your friend to get help and make yourself available to help them, but it is their choice, and you need to respect their decisions. This can be very difficult as the support person to recognize an abusive relationship and be unable to help someone you care about the way you want to. Support people and bystanders need to access support, too, because they are also impacted by witnessing abusive behaviors.

SEXUAL ASSAULT AND RAPE

The disturbing truth is that sexual assault and rape are *far* more common than many women realize. It's a huge issue for us (and we do mean all of us—this involves women *and* men, as perpetrators and as victims) as a society, as well as an issue that is especially relevant during your time at school.

This is a critical period in women's lives: College women between the ages of 18 and 24 are three times more likely to experience sexual violence than other women (Rape, Abuse and Incest National Network n.d.a). And sexual violence on campus is pervasive: 26.4% of undergraduate women experience rape or sexual assault through physical force, violence, or incapacitation ("Campus Sexual Violence: Statistics" n.d.)

Defining Key Terms

Just to be clear going forward, let's define some key terms (according to the definitions provided by RAINN—the Rape, Abuse and Incest National Network). Also important to note: Every state has a different *legal* definition for "sexual assault," as opposed to "rape"—and schools also have different definitions for what constitutes "sexual misconduct."

◊ **Sexual assault:** "sexual contact or behavior that occurs without explicit consent of the victim," including penetration of the victim's body, attempted rape, or forcing a victim to perform sexual acts (Rape, Abuse and Incest National Network n.d.c).

◊ **Rape:** "a form of sexual assault" and a term often used as a "legal definition to specifically include sexual penetration without consent" (Rape, Abuse and Incest National Network n.d.c).

It's also important to note that both rape and sexual assault are **nonconsensual**. Consent—when both parties agree to the act—is the key to what differentiates "sex" from "rape" or "sexual assault."

What You Need to Know

Young women are often led to believe that sexual assault or rape happens in dark alleys to girls who are "wasted" or look "slutty" by nefarious strangers. Basically, every part of that sentence is hardly true (and is all kinds of messed up), so let's take a second to unpack it and discuss what sexual assault is more likely to look like.

The perpetrator: Approximately 80% of sexual assaults are committed by someone known to the victim (Rape, Abuse and Incest National Network n.d.d). The bottom line is that rape is rape: It is forced sexual intercourse. It has nothing to do with whether or not the two people are in a relationship, how long they've known each other, or anything else. The act stands alone. And unfortunately, it's an act that perpetrators often get away with—only 25 out of every 1,000 rapists will be incarcerated (Rape, Abuse and Incest National Network n.d.b).

The "victim": First and foremost, we need to address that some people feel that calling somebody who has been raped a "victim" only revictimizes her (or him—it's important to remember that at least one in six men in the United States has been sexually abused) and many people who have been raped prefer to be called "survivors" ("The 1 in 6 Statistic" n.d.).

Secondly, we need to talk about victim blaming. Far too many survivors (especially female survivors) who speak out are doubted, asked what they were wearing, or if they did anything to cause it. The knowledge of such victim blaming keeps many women from telling anybody about the rape at all, which may prevent many from seeking the best path to justice. As for men, we live in a culture that, for myriad reasons (such as hypermasculinity standards, for example), tries to deny and/or erase the reality of male survivors of sexual assault and/or violence. Thus, men often don't speak out, either.

Bottom line: It's essential to put the blame not on the person who was raped but on the *rapist*—where it belongs. We don't need to teach people how to *prevent* rape (especially in terms of what women specifically wear and how much they should drink). We need to teach *rapists* not to rape in the first place.

A really key part of changing the conversation surrounding rape and rape culture is to change the conception that people (especially women) should constantly be on guard and policing their partners by telling them "no," to the idea that both partners should only proceed if they hear an enthusiastic *yes*. This is known as "enthusiastic consent" and is at the heart of any healthy approach to a sexual relationship…and yet it's not exactly something taught in sex ed across the country (or in the cultural zeitgeist generally). Yet there are *so* many benefits to promoting enthusiastic consent, like:

◊ **Taking the burden/blame off women:** We live in a victim-blaming culture. When women are sexually assaulted, the first question we ask is, "Did *she* say no? What did *she* do to provoke her attacker?" Beyond being mind-numbingly infuriating that it's actually a thing to hold a person accountable for a horrible thing done *to* them, this idea perpetuates the idea that men are sexually uncontrollable and that it's women's duty to reign them in and not provoke them in any way—a notion highly insulting to women as well as men. Enthusiastic consent should be about partners making an agreement—it involves them *both*.

◊ **Making the situation very clear:** "Gray rape" is a phrase that has been circulating for years and refers to the situation in which a partner may not have specifically said "no" but didn't express consent, either. Let's be very clear: If a rape occurs, it should not be blamed on a woman's lack of clarity. The idea of enthusiastic consent is that *everybody* involved can be *very clear* about what they want and what they're going to do before they do it, especially and primarily men. Enthusiastic consent teaches men to only act in terms of gaining (and continuously confirming) consent and, therefore, (ideally) changes the mindset with which both partners enter a sexual encounter.

◊ **Setting the mood:** There's a pesky rumor that enthusiastic consent "kills the mood"—it takes you outside yourself and out of the moment. But we would argue that it's actually a total turn on. You're both agreeing that, *yes*, you both *really* want to have sex with each other. Also, until rape doesn't persist at a disturbingly high rate, the argument can be made that beyond "killing the mood," explicitly consenting—and teaching men to *only* act upon having an indication of enthusiastic consent—is just culturally necessary.

What to Do If You Have Been Sexually Assaulted or Raped

Hopefully, you never have to use this information, but it is *essential* to know should you have to.

◊ First, if you're not sure whether or not you have been raped or sexually assaulted, RAINN has an excellent online hotline of trained staff who can help you work through the incident, which can be accessed at hotline.rainn.org.

◊ It can often take victims days, weeks, months, or even longer to recognize what happened—especially if they were assaulted by a partner. If you recognize that you have been assaulted immediately after the fact, though, do not shower, change your clothes, or even eat, drink, wash your hands, or brush your teeth to save all physical evidence of the assault. Go to the hospital or your campus's health center as soon as possible to receive care and have a rape kit done. Even if you don't want to pursue legal action, it's a good idea to collect evidence so that you have the option.

◊ If you think you might want to pursue legal action, report the incident to the police as soon as possible. Report and/ or write down everything you can remember about the incident. Keep in mind, though, that you are not obligated to report this incident or involve the legal system—many survivors who have gone to the police have encountered victim blaming from individual officers, as well as an overarching legal system inadequately resourced to help them, and have not found that process helpful.

◊ Do not keep the incident to yourself just because you think people will blame you or be ashamed of you. That's that victim-blaming mentality at play. The people who love you will always love you and will want to do all they can to help you. Do not let the incident shame you into silence if you want to speak out.

◊ Take care of yourself. Call a rape crisis center, find a counselor, and surround yourself with loved ones. Do everything and anything possible to get the help and support you need.

How to Help a Friend Who Was Sexually Assaulted or Raped

◊ If you witness the actual incident (or even acts leading up to it), resist the bystander effect. As mentioned in the earlier section on dating violence, people are less likely to intervene in a situation between two people who know each other, especially between those they know are in a relationship, but it's always better to be safe than sorry. If you think something is wrong between two people, it's always worth risking social awkwardness to double-check that everything's okay.

◊ If a friend tells you she was sexually assaulted or raped, help her carefully weigh her options for action. Some rape survivors do not want to deal with their rapists again—they want to avoid the heavy emotional process of confronting their rapist and reliving the trauma of the incident and are aware that the legal systems and campus adjudication processes in place often work against survivors. That may be valid, but it's also worth considering the consequences of doing nothing. It's entirely possible that a rapist is likely to be a repeat offender, and speaking out could save others from having the same experience.

◊ Generally, try to put your friend at ease, validate their experience, help guide them through the aforementioned steps, and refer to resources like the guide on the organization Know Your IX's website (http://knowyourix.org). Essentially, once you've made sure that your friend gets the help she needs and is in contact with professionals and people with more authority, your job is to be there for her. She'll need support, and being able to offer it in abundance is one of the best things you can do for her.

What You Need to Know About Title IX

Students have multiple reporting options in the aftermath of an assault: They can report it to the police, their school, or both (or neither). The police respond to rape as a crime, and reporting this crime can ultimately involve a criminal trial and potential jail time for a perpetrator. Schools that receive federal funding (which is the majority of schools), on the other hand, must comply with a federal statute called Title IX, which prohibits sex discrimination in education, including sexual harassment, gender-based discrimination, and sexual violence, and therefore affects how they respond to students' reports of sexual harassment and violence.

Under Title IX, schools must respond to and address hostile educational environments; failure to do so could mean risking losing federal funding. For years, Title IX was used as a tool to help student survivors, but in 2020, the U.S. Department of Education's new Title IX rule went into effect and rolled back protections for student survivors and reduced schools' obligations to prevent and respond to sexual harassment and assault ("Know Your IX" n.d.)

Every school can have its own policies outside of Title IX, though, so it's important to know what your school's sexual misconduct policy is to determine if it could still help to report.

SEXUAL VIOLENCE RESOURCES

These organizations and websites offer more information about sexual violence and how to move forward and potentially take action in the wake of experiencing sexual abuse, harassment, or violence.

- ◆ **Know Your IX** (http://knowyourix.org): This is a survivor- and youth-led project of Advocates for Youth that aims to empower students to end sexual and dating violence in their schools.
- ◆ **The American Association of University Women** (AAUW; www.aauw.org): The AAUW is also dedicated to fighting sexual misconduct in schools and offers resources and ways to take action.
- ◆ **Rape, Abuse & Incest National Network** (RAINN; www.rainn.org): RAINN is the largest anti-sexual violence organization in the U.S. and offers National Sexual Assault Hotlines: 800.656.HOPE (phone) and hotline.rainn.org (chat). The organization also has an abundance of helpful resources and information on its website.

REFERENCES

"The 1 in 6 Statistic." n.d. Sexual Abuse & Assault of Boys & Men | Confidential Support for Men. https://1in6.org/statistic/.

"Be More than a Bystander." n.d. Ending Violence BC. https://endingviolence.org/bystander/.

Beaudry, Kayleigh M., Izabella A. Ludwa, Aysha M. Thomas, Wendy E. Ward, Bareket Falk, and Andrea R. Josse. 2019. "First-Year University Is Associated With Greater Body Weight, Body Composition and Adverse Dietary Changes in Males Than Females." Edited by David Meyre. *PLOS ONE* 14(7). https://doi.org/10.1371/journal.pone.0218554.

Bowe, Kristen. 2023. "College Students and Depression." Mayo Clinic Health System. August 22. www.mayoclinichealthsystem.org/hometown-health/speaking-of-health/college-students-and-depression.

Brody, Debra, Laura Pratt, and Jeffery Hughes. 2018. "Prevalence of Depression Among Adults Aged 20 and Over: United States, 2013—2016." Centers for Disease Control and Prevention. www.cdc.gov/nchs/products/databriefs/db303.htm#print.

"Campus Sexual Violence: Statistics." n.d. RAINN. www.rainn.org/statistics/campus-sexual-violence.

Centers for Disease Control and Prevention. 2022a. "STD Facts—Human Papillomavirus (HPV)." April 12. www.cdc.gov/std/HPV/STDFact-HPV.htm.

Centers for Disease Control and Prevention. 2022b. "Alcohol Use and Your Health." April 14. www.cdc.gov/alcohol/fact-sheets/alcohol-use.htm.

Centers for Disease Control and Prevention. 2023b. "Detailed STD Facts—Chlamydia." April 12. www.cdc.gov/std/chlamy dia/stdfact-chlamydia-detailed.htm.

Cleveland Clinic. 2022. "Masturbation: Facts & Benefits." October 25. https://my.clevelandclinic.org/health/articles/ 24332-masturbation.

Dold, Kristen, Jasmine Gomez, Ashley Mateo, and Ashley Martens. 2022. "3 Common Causes of Sudden, Unexplained Weight Gain, According to Doctors." Women's Health Magazine. Spring 22. www.womenshealthmag.com/health/a19992956/ unexplained-weight-gain/.

Jacobson, Rae. 2023. "College Students and Eating Disorders." Child Mind Institute. February 8. https://childmind.org/arti cle/eating-disorders-and-college/.

Johns Hopkins Medicine. 2020. "Genital Herpes." www.hopk insmedicine.org/health/conditions-and-diseases/herpes-hsv1- and-hsv2/genital-herpes.

"Know Your IX: What to Know About the Title IX Rule." n.d. Knowyourix.org. https://knowyourix.org/hands-off-ix/basics/.

Love Is Respect. 2020. "Types of Abuse." Love Is Respect. www. loveisrespect.org/resources/types-of-abuse/.

National Institute of Mental Health. 2023. "Depression." National Institute of Mental Health. April. www.nimh.nih.gov/health/ topics/depression.

National Institute on Alcohol Abuse and Alcoholism. n.d. "Alcohol Calorie Calculator—Rethinking Drinking." Rethinking Drinking. National Institutes of Health. http://rethinkingd rinking.niaaa.nih.gov/toolsresources/caloriecalculator.asp.

Nawaz, Amna, and Diane Lincoln Estes. 2022. "People of Color With Eating Disorders Face Cultural, Medical Stigmas." PBS NewsHour. March 28. www.pbs.org/newshour/show/people- of-color-with-eating-disorders-face-cultural-medical-stigmas.

NVRDC. 2020. "#DVAM2020: Domestic & Dating Violence on College and University Campuses." Network for Victim Recovery of DC. October 30. www.nvrdc.org/blog/2020/10/30/dvam2020-domestic-amp-dating-violence-on-college-and-university-campuses#_ftn1.

Planned Parenthood. n.d. "STDs and STIs." Planned Parenthood Mar Monte. www.plannedparenthood.org/planned-parenthood-mar-monte/campaigns/stds-stis.

Rape, Abuse and Incest National Network. (n.d.a). "Victims of Sexual Violence: Statistics." www.rainn.org/statistics/victims-sexual-violence.

Rape, Abuse and Incest National Network. (n.d.b). "The Criminal Justice System: Statistics." www.rainn.org/get-information/statistics/reporting-rates.

Rape, Abuse and Incest National Network. (n.d.c). "Sexual Assault." www.rainn.org/articles/sexual-assault.

Rape, Abuse and Incest National Network. (n.d.d). "Perpetrators of Sexual Violence: Statistics." www.rainn.org/statistics/perpetrators-sexual-violence.

Stalking Prevention, Awareness, and Resource Center. n.d. "Stalking Among College Students: Fact Sheet." www.stalkingawareness.org/wp-content/uploads/2021/09/Campus-Stalking-Fact-Sheet.pdf.

CHAPTER 5

LET'S TALK ABOUT DEBT, BABY

Funding a college education is not just the first big financial decision most women make but also one of the most impactful—it's one of the biggest investments most people ever make.

And yet, if you're anything like us, when you hear words like "financial" or "investment," your limbs slowly grow heavy, your eyes glaze over, and your mind begins to turn off. We're hardly the only girls ignorant about the nitty-gritty of financial responsibility, even at the cusp of adulthood, either.

To be fair, finance—or handling money in any real way—is a historically male-dominated industry, personal responsibility, and topic of conversation. Until relatively recently, women had no access to their own money and remained completely financially dependent on men; women were passed from their fathers to their husbands, literally considered property in the eyes of the law. Women who didn't marry were considered a burden on their families and were often left destitute without their families' help.

But despite having come so far from having the financial autonomy of a toaster, far too many young women are still largely uneducated about money—or at least are not encouraged

 DOI: 10.4324/9781003408932-5

Women and Finance

Because our generation was largely told we're equal to our brothers and guy friends, many of us don't realize just how recently our rights were won. But the truth is that history informs everything that happens in the present, and the way women approach money is no exception. Here are just a few reminders of how recent some of women's economic rights are:

♦ **The Declaration of Sentiments and Resolutions**, created at the Seneca Falls Convention in 1848, called for an end to laws that denied married women control of any money and/or property (among other things, it was one of the first times American women formally fought for legal, economic, and social autonomy).

♦ More than 100 years later, in 1963, the **Equal Pay Act** was passed, making it illegal for men to make more money than women for equal work. It's worth noting that, despite this legislation, women still only make about 82 cents to every man's dollar—a figure that's even lower for women of color (Kochhar 2023).

♦ **The Equal Credit Opportunity Act** was passed in 1974 and made it illegal for creditors to deny somebody a credit card based on gender, race, religion, marital status, etc.

♦ Before the **Women's Business Ownership Act** passed in 1988, some states still legally required women to have a male relative cosign their loan for anything from a business to a car to a home, even if they were employed and financially qualified. Let's just emphasize that: Less than *40 years ago*, women couldn't get their own loans in some places.

to learn about it the way our male counterparts are. Yet, we're expected to make one of the biggest financial decisions of our lives as teenagers. And how we decide to pay for school has the ability to shape our entire lives—for better and for much, much worse.

First, the better: A college degree will help you earn more money over the course of your career. Workers with bachelor's degrees earn 62% more than those whose highest level of education is a high school diploma—and that figure is closer to 90% for workers with graduate degrees (Cuellar Mejia et al. 2023). The unemployment rate is also lower for college graduates than for workers without bachelor's degrees (Schaeffer 2022).

But then there's the devastating and potentially life-altering reality of student debt. Over 43 million Americans (20% of all American adults) have student loan debt, and that debt has surpassed a total of more than $1.7 trillion (Hanson 2023b). The number of student borrowers in this country is also only increasing, as are tuition costs—the average student loan debt growth rate outpaces rising tuition costs by 166.9% (Hanson 2023b).

What's more, women are disproportionately represented among student loan debt holders. Women comprise 61.4% of bachelor's degree holders with federal student loans, and women with bachelor's degrees borrow 4.27% more in loans than their male peers (Hanson 2023b). This trend holds among associate's degree holders, too: Women students are 49.9% more likely to borrow federal student loans, and they borrow 24.9% more loans than their male peers (Hanson 2023b).

So what's the best course of action? Although wishing for a Student Loan Fairy Godmother to descend from Higher Education Heaven and supply you with endless amounts of liquid cash is one (wildly optimistic) strategy, another is to thoroughly educate yourself about your college payment options and prudently pick the one that's best for you—and to stay vigilant about your options and the state of your debt throughout your entire time at college.

Because we would never wish upon you the hell that is wading through the convoluted and boring information about student loans out there, we will now present you with this, your *Smart Girl's Guide to Paying for College Without Incurring Crippling Debt That Destroys Your Life.*

GIVE IT TO ME STRAIGHT: YOUR BASIC OPTIONS

The hard truth is that the best way to approach college financially is to start early—like much earlier than right before you head off to college. Ideally, you will have been born an heiress to the Hostess fortune (access to money and, I can only presume, unlimited, delicious baked goods full of hydrogenated fat—it's the dream). If you were born a mere plebe, you would have gotten straight As, cured cancer, qualified for the Olympic badminton team, saved all of the stray puppies in your hometown, and, if you found a spare minute, perhaps won first prize in the county fair for your scrumptious apple pie (you know, on a whim). Thus, you will be a shoo-in for athletic, academic, merit, and culinary (if they exist?) scholarships and will be flush with other generous souls' cash.

If accomplishing all those things wasn't realistic for you, first take a good, hard look at your life because you are *clearly* a hopeless failure. After you thoroughly shame yourself for failing to achieve a combination of goals before the end of your teens that would take a gaggle of grown adults their entire lifetimes to accomplish, take a deep breath and consider these options.

SCHOLARSHIPS

Even if you're not the world's most perfect teen, you still have a shot at getting a scholarship. Scholarships award students free money; they don't require repayment and thus help you avoid debt by keeping your financial responsibilities and culpabilities to a minimum. And they may be more attainable than you think: More than $6 billion in scholarships are awarded to college students each year, and around one in eight college students has won one (Nova 2023).

The downside: The average scholarship award is around $4,200, and only around 0.1% of undergraduate students receive $25,000 or more in scholarships, so they're unlikely to fund an entire education (Nova 2023). But, to emphasize: FREE. MONEY. There are zero drawbacks to applying for as many scholarships as you can. Although you should ideally start applying for them during your senior year of high school (if not earlier), many scholarships are offered on an ongoing basis. Because most scholarships are only valid for a single academic year anyway, you can (and should) keep applying throughout your college career.

Here are some basic scholarship tips:

◇ **There's a scholarship out there for everybody:** Although many people believe scholarships are only available for the next LeBron James or Marie Curie, there are actually plenty of scholarships out there that have no GPA, athletic, or other achievement-based requirements; many are granted based on financial need. If you have no hand-eye coordination or have math class-specific narcolepsy, there is hope for you yet. Or, if you have a unique talent or background, you may be eligible for a very specific scholarship. In either case, try using scholarship search and match tools, like Fastweb (http://fastweb.com) and Scholarships.com (http://scholarships.com), which match you with scholarships you're eligible for based on your particular background and needs.

◇ **Even small awards add up:** Many people feel so defeated by the enormous amount of tuition facing them that they don't bother applying for scholarships in the $1,000 to

$5,000 range and instead focus on going for the giant, all-encompassing prizes. MISTAKE. Even if you only win a single $1,000 scholarship, that's a grand more than you had to begin with. That money could cover your books and other various fees for the year. Every cent counts.

◊ **Beware of scholarship displacement:** Some colleges reduce the financial aid they offer students based on the scholarships they receive via a practice called "scholarship displacement." Five states—California, Maryland, New Jersey, Pennsylvania, and Washington—have banned scholarship displacement, so if you're going to school in those states, you're set. If you're going to school elsewhere, it's important to be aware of your college's policy if you've received financial aid and are also applying for scholarships.

◊ **Use your scholarship wisely to avoid taxes:** Scholarships are taxable if you use them for anything other than tuition and books (including room and board or other living expenses). To keep the full amount of your scholarship, you'll want to put it toward those expenses.

ASK AN EXPERT

Scholarships

Don't be afraid to ask questions, whether it's to a financial aid officer, one of your mentors, or someone else on campus. When I was in college, I was shy and didn't want to ask about scholarships, but I ended up getting a small scholarship just by reaching out and asking someone in the financial aid office. For women, speaking up and advocating for ourselves is really important, and you never know what you're going to find.

—Sabrina Calazans, Managing Director of the Student Debt Crisis Center

WORKING

In the face of thousands upon thousands of dollars, attempting to earn enough money to make a dent in tuition can seem futile. And it's true: While our parents and grandparents may have been able to work their way through college, it's just not possible for many students today to earn enough money during the summers or between classes to put themselves through school.

That being said, just like with scholarships, every dollar counts. Even if working doesn't completely cover your tuition, it will likely help—not to mention that other costs, like books, add up. You'll also want money to buy food, go out with friends, and live a little. Working can help with that.

But I am just barely an adult and have few marketable skills, you may be thinking to yourself. *What am I to do to earn some meager wages?* Well, there are some classic options:

◊ **Service industries:** It's common knowledge that if you can survive the ridiculous demands, rudeness, and sometimes straight-up stupidity of customers in the retail or food service industries, you have developed a marketable and vital life skill. Seriously, serving people to their satisfaction is *not easy* and is actually something future employers recognize as such and thus love to see on your résumé because it says a lot about your character. Also, in retail, you often get an employee discount, so, you know, score.

◊ **Babysitting or nannying:** It's undeniably a stereotypical choice for girls, and if you have the urge to yell, "CHILDREN YOUR AGE ARE DYING FROM MALARIA," every time your precious charges throw tantrums over still slightly frozen chicken nuggets, it may not be the right option for you. But if you have that maternal gene, it's pretty easy to find work, pays well, and generally pays in cash (which means no taxes). Plus, if you play it right, you can make the children your loyal minions.

◊ **Start your own business:** Are you an expert bead craftswoman? Do your knitted shawls rival your Amish grandmother's? Sell them! SELL THEM ALL. With the rise of marketplace apps, there are plenty of ways to make your fabulous creations widely available for purchase. Also, if you have skills that don't translate directly into a concrete product—like if you're a graphic designer, bilingual, or a real-life guitar hero—don't be afraid to market your skills. Post on social media and spread the word in your community that you're available to tutor or redesign a website. Young women today abound with marketable skills—we're just rarely clued into the fact that we can (and should) capitalize on them.

OUT OF THE MOUTHS OF ~~BABES~~ CURRENT COLLEGE STUDENTS

Working Through School

If you are someone like me who worked to pay for school, it's a good idea to reach out to your professors and/or academic advisor if you are struggling to balance a schedule composed of both work and school. Although some professors may not seem the most approachable, it is important to vocalize your experiences because they are valid. Oftentimes, professors can also make accommodations for you to where you feel more comfortable with the workload and time constraints you have."

—Neha, University of Texas at Austin

FINANCIAL AID

We hate to break it to you, but no matter how vehemently college admissions officers swear up and down that they are need-blind and will meet all demonstrated need, their definition of "demonstrated need" has historically not been one that reasonable human beings can get behind. The Free Application for Federal Student Aid (FAFSA) form that you submit with your college application evaluates how much aid is recommended for a school to award you for a single year. The college then uses this expected contribution to evaluate how much aid they'll give you, which could include straight-up money, a work-study program, or recommended loans.

At the end of the day, though, there are a few basic issues with relying on (or expecting to rely on) financial aid, even if you do consider yourself financially needy.

◇ **The FAFSA form can fail to capture the financial reality of you and/or your family:** The thing about this system is that numbers on paper hardly tell the full story of what your family can actually expect to put toward your education. It's not uncommon for schools to determine that you *technically* have enough money to pay for a certain amount of tuition every year—not taking into account the fact that your parents need to help out your grandparents, save for your siblings' education, or any number of financial scenarios not captured by a form. Or maybe you don't qualify for financial aid at all, but your family doesn't have the kind of money necessary to fund an entire college education lying around. Ultimately, the FAFSA's determination of "need" has been pretty out of touch with the financial reality of many (if not most) families.

The FAFSA has recently undergone some changes, however. The FAFSA for the 2024–2025 school year was reduced from 108 questions to just 36 and more easily imports income data from tax records. The Department of Education also announced it would change its formulas to determine who qualifies for aid and how much they receive.

◇ **Your financial aid package could change every year:** Let's say that miraculously, you get an amazing aid package to the school of your dreams. *Huzzah*, you think to yourself, *a prosperous future is within grasp!* You attend your sickeningly expensive dream school for a fraction of the cost. You're on top of the world. Then, upon receiving your sophomore aid package, you realize it isn't quite as generous. *All right*, you think, *I'll just pick up a few extra shifts. It'll be fine.* You manage. Then your junior year comes around, and you're sure there has been a clerical error: that extra 0 does *not* belong at the end of your expected contribution. How are you going to pay?

Many colleges "frontload" their financial aid packages: They give students a solid financial aid package their first year and then reduce it in subsequent years. You've already invested in the school, financially and personally, so you feel obligated to make it work by taking out extra loans or doing whatever else you need to when you probably could've gotten an overall cheaper education at a different school. Just add this to the list of ways some schools (*especially* private schools) try to screw you over.

If you want to go to college and can't pay out of pocket, you'll need to jump through the financial aid hoops. Just make sure to read the fine print of your financial aid package or, better yet, ask your college directly if they practice frontloading grants in their financial aid packages. You can also use College Navigator (nces.ed.gov/collegenavigator), a U.S. Department of Education tool, to compare the amount of financial aid given to freshmen versus overall undergraduate students at your school.

◇ **You can appeal for more financial aid:** If your family is experiencing an unusual financial circumstance—such as a reduction in income due to job loss, financial burdens from medical bills, unexpected expenses for caring for senior family members, or a number of other situations—you can write a financial aid appeal letter. Contact your school's financial aid office and ask them about their requirements for making an appeal. Then, determine how much aid you need to ask for, provide documentation that backs up your family's changed financial circumstances, and submit an appeal explaining your situation.

TO OFFER MY TIME AND LABOR FOR FREE OR NOT (THE INTERNING DEBATE)

♦ At some point in your college career, you'll likely realize the Catch-22 of postgrad employment: many employers want candidates—even those applying for entry-level positions—to already have work experience. Even though it's impossible to get that experience without a job. Which you can't get unless you already have experience.

♦ Enter internships, which offer opportunities to get that work experience but are all too often unpaid. Most college freshmen aren't concerned with getting (or expected to get) an internship, but it's something to keep in mind for the years to come—and to consider carefully.

♦ *Pros:* Internships let you explore your possible career interests, allowing you to rule out a path if you find you hate it or help you narrow your academic interests toward a certain career route. Internships also often facilitate making connections that may lead to a job down the road.

♦ *Cons:* Because so many are unpaid, internships require you to offer a significant amount of your time (and life) for basically the vague promise of an advantage down the line. Also, most internship programs expect *very* little of their charges, allowing them to create basic Excel sheets or grab coffee, which can be really frustrating and boring.

If you decide you want to intern, check in with your campus's career resources (including a designated center or office, listserv, career fairs, or alumni networks). Not only could your college help you find an internship, but it may also have funds available to support students' unpaid internships.

And, really, you should be compensated for your time and effort. There's a lot of pressure to take any internship offered—paid or not—but know that no matter what you decide, your work has value, and there should be a limit to how much you do for free.

TAKING OUT LOANS

Student loans are like any other loans in the most basic sense: You borrow money from a lender with the understanding that you will repay what you borrowed plus interest. And for the majority of students, there's just no way to get a college education without taking out a loan. In fact, nearly 64% of 2021 graduates had borrowed money (Kerr and Wood 2022).

There are a few types of student loans (see Table 5.1), which is good in the sense that choices are always welcome and horrible in that these options can be overwhelming and confusing, and can lead to some seriously bad choices. Having solid information goes a long way toward making smart decisions, though, so here is a basic guide to your student loan options.

Federal Student Loans

Overall, a federal loan—either a Direct Subsidized Loan or a Direct Unsubsidized Loan—is the best option if you have to take out loans and is *absolutely* the way to go over private loans. Keep these things in mind if you get a federal loan:

◇ These loans are available through the United States Department of Education, and you must submit a FAFSA to access them.

Table 5.1

Main Types of Loans Available

Loan	Description	The Nitty-Gritty
Direct Subsidized Loan	Direct Subsidized Loans are federal student loans for undergraduate students on which the government pays the interest while you're in school.	These loans are determined by financial need, which is determined by information you provide in your application. Your school will determine the amount you can borrow, and that amount also depends on whether you're financially independent from your parents.
Direct Unsubsidized Loan	Direct Unsubsidized Loans are federal student loans for undergraduate, graduate, and professional students on which you are charged interest while in school.	You don't need to demonstrate financial need to get this loan; your school determines the amount you can borrow based on the cost of attendance and other aid you receive. If you don't make interest payments while in school, the interest will be added to the loan amount each year and result in a larger balance when you graduate.
Direct PLUS Loan	Direct PLUS Loans can be taken out by a parent or grandparent to help pay for additional costs not covered by other loans or aid.	These loans have higher interest rates, but the interest is tax deductible. The maximum amount you can receive is the remaining cost of your tuition.
Private Loan	Private loans are available from banks, credit unions, and online lenders.	Private loans have variable interest rates (which means they can change at any time while you still have the loan) and don't come with borrower protections that federal loans have.

◇ Federal loan interest rates are set by federal law and are typically lower than private loan rates.

For more information on all types of federal loans, visit the U.S. Department of Education's website: http://studentaid.gov. Also, check out tools like this loan calculator, which helps you estimate how big your loan payments will be and the type of salary you'll need to make those payments after graduation: http://finaid.org/calculators/loanpayments.

Private Student Loans

Private student loans are the devil. They are provided primarily by banks and credit unions and are issued to students who have exhausted all other financial options and are still not able to handle the cost of college. Private loans have variable interest rates (which means they can change at any time while you still have the loan) and non-standardized repayment schedules (which makes it harder to budget for paying off the loan).

Seriously, if you find yourself in a situation where you can only afford a certain college by taking out a private loan, you should consider attending a different school. Being able to call yourself a Bobcat/Panther/Tiger/Other Exotic Cat is definitely not worth financial ruin.

REPAYING LOANS

Countless college grads have horror stories that go something like this: Feeling overwhelmed by an abundance of financial speak and lack of thorough knowledge and research, they signed on the dotted line for a loan at 18 that resulted in them owing considerably more than the cost of their college tuition thanks to interest and/or defaulting (not being able to make loan payments). Far too many college grads today lead lives generally dictated by crippling debt—opting not to start families, unable to become homeowners or start their own businesses, and laughing at the idea of actually following their dreams—all based on a decision they made *literally* before their frontal lobe was fully developed.

So let's talk about repaying loans. First, why do so many Americans struggle to pay their student loans? Well, the fact that college tuition has increased 747.8% since 1963 (you read that right) has something to do with it (Hanson 2023c). Every year, students are forced to take out larger and larger loans that result in larger and larger monthly repayment fees, yet the monthly earnings of an average grad are hardly keeping up; the average student loan debt per borrower is $40,114, yet the median starting salary among all new graduates is $61,600 (Hanson 2023a). This results in the average student borrower taking *20 years* to pay off their student loan debt (Hanson 2021).

Among graduates who are able to make their monthly loan payments, fewer can afford to do anything else with their money, such as making significant investments, which in turn impedes their ability to build wealth or, you know, fulfill their dreams. In fact, a 2022 survey found that 81% of people with student loans said they delayed at least one major life milestone, such as buying a home or having a baby, because of their debt (Hess 2022).

And then there are those who simply can't make their loan payments. Fifteen percent of Americans with student loans are behind on their payments, and over a million student loans enter default each year, which affects nine million borrowers and their families (Caporal 2023; Hanson 2021). As if that weren't bad enough, borrowers who have defaulted are punished with life-altering penalties like bad credit scores that make getting any other loans (like for a house or car) impossible, losing the professional licenses for which they went into debt in the first place (the ultimate, ironic bitch of a Catch-22), and even opening themselves up to being sued for their loan's value.

Those consequences of defaulting are possible because consumer protections have been removed from student loans. For example, although declaring bankruptcy is a viable option for anybody else in debt (including gamblers, for instance), those with student loan debt can't declare bankruptcy. In fact, federal student debt collectors can collect debt from a borrower's wages and income tax refunds. Although other indebted individuals can refinance their loans to make payments more manageable, those with student debt aren't able to refinance.

So, what can you do now to make repaying your loans more manageable later?

◇ **Carefully consider repayment plans:** There are four main types of repayment plans for federal loans: standard repayment (lasts ten years), graduated repayment (starts low and then increases the amount you pay every two years for a total of ten years), income-driven repayment (ties the amount you pay to a portion of your income), and extended repayment (starts payments low then increases every two years for a total of 25 years). Generally, the lowest starting payments will be on extended repayment and income-driven repayment, while the highest will be on standard repayment and graduated repayment. The lower your payments, though, the more interest you'll pay over the life of the loan. So you'll pay the least interest overall if you go with a standard repayment plan and the most if you go with an extended repayment plan.

◇ **Take your professional plans into consideration:** Yes, the world is your oyster, and you have plenty of time to figure out what color your parachute is, but it's worth at least making a basic assessment of what salary range you're aiming for to determine what size loan repayments you'll realistically be able to make once you graduate. For example, if you know you want to be a teacher (or some other heroic and absolutely vital profession that is grossly undervalued and underpaid), you are in for a world of pain if you decide to attend an elite school that has offered you very little financial aid. But, then again, if investment banking is your calling…well, we have nothing in common, but it may actually make sense to go into debt for an Ivy League education, since those are virtually the only schools elite investment banks recruit from, and if all goes according to plan, you'll probably pay off your debt in a few years (for the reasonable price of thousands of dollars + your soul, but whatever).

The bottom line about paying for college is this: The system is absolutely broken and desperately needs to be reformed, but there are ways to make informed, pragmatic decisions within the context of what is frankly a really bad situation. Of course, any financial decisions you make about paying for college should be discussed with your parents, a banker, or any other financial advisor you trust. But, because this is a guidebook and we are your self-appointed spiritual guides, we *do* have some tips:

Thoroughly research all of your options. This whole process is about education, right? Well, lucky for you, that starts before you even set foot in a classroom. Do your homework: Don't get lazy with your scholarship search, and take your time filing for financial aid. Those forms can be kind of tricky and convoluted, but don't let a clerical error keep you from cash. For example, be aware that your family should file their taxes early the year you apply for college because no college will finalize a financial aid package until you or your parents (if you're dependent) file current tax forms. If you go the loan route, make sure you talk to *multiple* people about what option makes the most sense for your financial situation.

Ask for advice, but take it with a grain of salt. Although you definitely shouldn't devise your entire plan for paying for college alone (because, come on, rising freshmen are like a half step removed from childhood and this is a huge responsibility), you also need to be aware of the varying interests of those advising you. For example, high school guidance counselors probably want you to choose the most elite (i.e., expensive) college possible and may steer you in that direction even if it doesn't financially make sense for you because it makes them look good. Admissions officers and other college representatives' jobs are to sell their college to you, and they could make claims or stretch the truth about financial aid and other financial opportunities to get you to buy in. Collegiate financial aid officers will do what they can to help you cover tuition…but it's not their place (and it's not in their interest) to advise you that you really can't afford to go to their school in the first place. And then there are family and friends who likely do have your complete best interest at heart but may not have the financial savvy to give you the help or advice you need. Your best bet is to do your own research and consider the advice offered by all of these people but ultimately make your *own* decision.

Don't rule out public schools and even community college— at least for a couple of years. If you're already preparing for your freshman year at a private college, this tip may be lost on you, and we certainly don't want to diss private schools (hell, we went to them). But from a strictly financial perspective, going to a public school (or, better yet, community college) is generally the best option in terms of avoiding debt (unless you're on a full ride or have some other kind of sweet deal). By definition, public colleges and universities are *publicly funded*, which means that state taxpayers contribute to the institution's costs. If you're looking at college like an investment, not just an experience, your ROI (return on investment) will likely be much higher at a public school because you'll have less debt working against your future earnings.

Also, although there is still a pretty pervasive stigma about attending community college from an academic and social perspective, financially, it's your best option. Even attending community college for your first year or two to knock out prerequisite classes (which are essentially the same everywhere) is advantageous. It's also a well-kept secret that you might be able to transfer to an even better school than you could originally have been admitted to by kicking ass at community college for a while. Many college admissions officers actually *recruit* transfers from high-performing community college students.

Make smart daily choices while at college. We need to talk about credit cards. Here's the thing: They are not magic. College students continuously get into credit card debt because they're not vigilant about curbing spending and paying off their balances. It doesn't help that banks target students for this very reason with student credit cards, which offer low credit limits, low-income requirements, and high interest rates, which equate to disaster. They are a trap and must be avoided at all costs. Getting a credit card is not a bad idea, though, because a super vital part of being an adult is having established (good) credit. If you do end up with a card, get one with a low limit and pay it off monthly like clockwork.

Also, make yourself a budget. At the risk of sounding like the Queens of the Funsuckers, do not leave anything to chance or spontaneity (unless you set aside some cash every month for the purpose of fun—yes, we're advocating for planned spontaneity). Deposit your monthly income into your savings account immediately and only allow yourself access to the money you allocated in your budget.

YOUR OTHER SYLLABUS

Important Student Loan Debt Reading Material

We are not experts on the topic of student loan debt, but luckily, there are a number of experts out there who have great advice—enough advice, in fact, to fill entire books! We highly recommend reading as many as you can, including:

◆ *The Debt Trap: How Student Loans Became a Natural Catastrophe by Josh Mitchell*: If you want to do a deep dive into how we ended up in the midst of a student loan debt crisis, this book takes you back to the 1950s and up through the present to reveal the many factors that contributed to the mess we're in.

◆ *The Price You Pay for College: An Entirely New Road Map for the Biggest Financial Decision Your Family Will Ever Make by Ron Lieber*: This book breaks down not only how to borrow and bargain for a better deal but also how to compare the price of a school with its value.

◆ *How to Appeal for More College Financial Aid by Mark Kantrowitz*: This book offers practical advice for negotiating a better financial aid offer.

Talking about debt is depressing, annoying, and boring. There's no way around that, and maybe that's why it's generally not something young women (or any college students) really talk about at length beyond a comment here or there lamenting how broke we all are and will be for some time. But it's a vitally important conversation to have. Financial stability is the foundation of our current and future success and happiness—on a personal level and (at the risk of overreaching) for our gender.

Why do young women pursue college degrees? Sure, some women go through the college process merely because they feel they're supposed to, and others are biding their time while waiting for somebody to come along and financially support them. But most young women go to college because they're pursuing their dreams and envision a bright future for themselves.

Most of our parents and other supportive forces in our lives encouraged us to go to college for that reason. "You can do anything you set your mind to!" they tell us. "Just work hard and believe in yourself, and anything is possible!" But while those types of warm and fuzzy sentiments are more than welcome (and in the context of a culture that constantly objectifies, sexualizes, and demeans young women, we could always use more of them), they also don't tell the whole story.

Vague rhetoric about girl power and believing in ourselves fails to account for the hard truth that we live in a patriarchal, capitalist society. Although many women may define success differently than men—while many of us consider healthy, solid relationships and fulfilling, purposeful work to mean success more than a certain salary or a high-ranking position of power—the truth is, there is a pervasive financial reality to success, happiness, and even just a basic, good quality of life that can't be ignored.

Women who want to start families and continue their careers, for example, will likely need daycare, which costs money (a lot of it). Starting a family in the first place is ridiculously hard to do if you're in debt or if you've defaulted—so is buying a house or starting your own business. At the end of the day, being able to pursue what we feel will make us successful and happy requires financial stability, which stems from the decisions we make about college.

Beyond being able to create the type of successful futures we want, though, we also need to be more transparent about financial literacy as an entire gender. The second wave of the feminist movement derived empowerment from a practice called *consciousness raising*. Groups of women would come together and discuss the problems they faced openly and honestly. In doing so, they realized that the issues they faced—everything from sexual violence to workplace discrimination to straight-up dissatisfaction—were not personal failures but larger, systemic issues affecting *all* women. Once they realized that they weren't alone, they banded together and were unstoppably powerful. We need to do a similar thing surrounding student debt on a vast scale, but also as women.

It's actually ridiculous when you think about it: So many of us are in the same boat and could derive support, strength, information, and financial strategies from each other if we would only openly discuss debt. So many young women who have taken out loans are only minimally educated about the types of loans they're saddled with and how those loans can and will impact them in the future. Many don't realize that their financial decision could lead to serious things like delaying motherhood and putting undue strain on their romantic relationships. Paying for college can potentially dictate one's life, and yet so many young women either don't realize this or simply accept it as inevitable.

Financial autonomy and responsibility are issues we undoubtedly need to own as women on the greater level of pursuing equality and success for our gender, but at the end of the day, it is an intimately personal thing. Figuring out how you're going to pay for college is the first truly huge and impactful decision you will make as an adult, and it's possible to make a smart decision that can lead to success and happiness. You are the *only* person who will answer for your debt. Feminist ideals aside, student loans and debt *necessitate* that you be strong, independent, savvy, and confident in yourself. Luckily, armed with comprehensive information, there's nothing stopping you from making financial choices that will set you up for a super successful and happy future.

REFERENCES

Caporal, Jack. 2023. "Student Loan Debt Statistics in 2023." The Motley Fool. August 1. www.fool.com/research/student-loan-debt-statistics/.

Cuellar Mejia, Marisol, Cesar Alesi Perez, Vicki Hsieh, and Hans Johnson. 2023. "Is College Worth It?" Public Policy Institute of California. March. www.ppic.org/publication/is-college-worth-it/.

Hanson, Melanie. 2021. "Average Time to Pay off Student Loans." Education Data Initiative. December 16. https://educationd ata.org/average-time-to-repay-student-loans.

Hanson, Melanie. 2023a. "Average Student Loan Payment." Education Data Initiative. May 30. https://educationdata.org/average-student-loan-payment.

Hanson, Melanie. 2023b. "Student Loan Debt Statistics." Education Data Initiative. July 17. https://educationdata.org/student-loan-debt-statistics.

Hanson, Melanie. 2023c. "College Tuition Inflation Rate." Education Data Initiative. August 13. https://educationdata.org/college-tuition-inflation-rate.

Hess, Abigail Johnson. 2022. "CNBC Survey: 81% of Adults With Student Loans Say They've Had to Delay Key Life Milestones." CNBC. January 28. www.cnbc.com/2022/01/28/81percent-of-adults-with-student-loans-say-they-delay-key-life-milesto nes.html.

Kerr, Emma, and Wood, Sarah. 2022. "See How Average Student Loan Debt Has Changed." U.S. News & World Report. September 13. www.usnews.com/education/best-colleges/pay ing-for-college/articles/see-how-student-loan-borrowing-has-changed.

Kochhar, Rakesh. 2023. "The Enduring Grip of the Gender Pay Gap." Pew Research Center's Social & Demographic Trends Project. March 1. www.pewresearch.org/social-trends/2023/03/01/the-enduring-grip-of-the-gender-pay-gap/https://www.pewresearch.org/social-trends/2023/03/01/the-enduring-grip-of-the-gender-pay-gap/.

Nova, Annie. 2023. "$6 Billion in College Scholarships Are Awarded Each Year. Here's What You Need to Know about Applying." CNBC. April 4. www.cnbc.com/2023/04/04/everything-students-need-to-know-about-college-scholarships.html.

Schaeffer, Katherine. 2022. "10 Facts about Today's College Graduates." Pew Research Center. April 12. www.pewresearch.org/short-reads/2022/04/12/10-facts-about-todays-college-graduate.

CHAPTER 6

ANIMAL HOUSE, SMART GIRL STYLE

Your social Life

When people talk about college, they generally don't tell the crazy story about the time they got an A in their Intro to Philosophy class. The go-to stories about (and general cultural conceptions of) college are usually related to its social aspects. It makes sense: College is an academic institution and a financial investment, but it's also a valuable opportunity to fully let loose, meet lifelong friends, and stockpile great stories. Frankly, it's an opportunity for fun that, especially in the context of our severely overworked and overstressed society, shouldn't be passed up.

 DOI: 10.4324/9781003408932-6

However, because it is such a distinctive experience, you'll soon learn that high school social norms largely do not apply. College is kind of like a sociological experiment: It's like boot camp for the real world (college students = adults in training), interspersed with a bunch of informal studies on human sexuality and the effects of alcohol on the brain. And, like most things in life, you'll likely find that your gender does make navigating these areas a unique endeavor, with specific rules to be aware of and serious pitfalls to avoid. But we have your back: Here's the essential guide to making the most of being social in college.

HOW SOCIALIZING CHANGES IN COLLEGE

Even if you managed to escape high school without feeling personally victimized by the designated queen bee of your high school, chances are if you are a teenager and you identify as female, you're well acquainted with the existence of "mean girls." For decades, high schools across the country have been plagued by girls who tear others down verbally and emotionally (and sometimes physically, but usually, the mind is the weapon of choice). There are plenty of experts who have intelligently deconstructed why some girls do this, but in the interest of moving on from high school and focusing on college, it's important to note that socializing in high school as a girl is different than it is in college.

"Different" is the key word. There seems to be a widespread misconception that college is a judgment-free wonderland of self-exploration and mutual understanding. Although everybody does chill out (like, a lot), that's, unfortunately, not quite the case. That type of all-encompassing acceptance and love really only exists in isolated hippie communes—and even then, there's probably some kind of drama about who is to blame for a disappointing hemp crop.

Bottom line: College students are humans, and humans need social structures. Popularity and cliques still exist—they just (thankfully) generally happen in a far more casual, low-pressure way and come from a place of positivity.

To be fair, though, socializing in college is hardly cut and dried. It varies from school to school and, like every other aspect of your college experience, depends on a number of variables. Here are just a few factors that may impact your college social experience:

◊ **School size:** If your college is essentially a city unto itself, then you're going to interact with your peers in a very different way than students at a rural liberal arts school that has a student body of a couple thousand. It seems that generally, the bigger the school, the more freewheeling you can be because people are hardly keeping track of you outside of your personal social network.

◊ **School location:** Schools often try to spin their locations into admissions pitches. *New York City is your backyard—there are so many professional and cultural opportunities!* NYU and Columbia admissions officers parrot over and over again. *This is a* real, authentic *college town—do your college experience right!* the University of Michigan insists about Ann Arbor. *Enjoy being sequestered by miles and miles of forest—what other school has a student body so diverse it includes feral squirrels and other woodland creatures?* said probably no admissions tour guide at Bard ever. But they often leave out that your school's location will inevitably impact your social life.

◊ If you do go to school in the middle of nowhere, chances are you'll be seeing the same people over and over again and will form a relatively tight-knit (and, on the downside, increasingly incestuous) community. If you're in a huge city, there are uniquely urban obstacles that prevent a cohesive community, like the dispersion of students into the city to seek out "real" bars or cultural activities (not to mention the lack of actual, physical space available for parties). But then again, there's an endless supply of new people and experiences in huge, dynamic cities. Neither social experience is necessarily better—they're just very different and cater to different students.

◇ **School type:** Going to a historically women's college is going to radically impact your social life. Although a lot of skeptics tend to incredulously wonder how you'll *ever survive* without guys around, and it's undeniable that the sheer lack of testosterone is a pretty informative social factor, most women's college students don't necessarily view the absence of men as the major catastrophe that some assume it is. Sure, it's nice to have guys around as friends, as well as romantic interests for those who are straight. But being in a community of women is also an empowering, comforting, and unique experience that simply can't be replicated elsewhere. And though we can't personally vouch for other types of specialized schools (like engineering schools or design/arts-based schools, for example), you can inevitably expect a somewhat different social experience at those schools, too.

And there are countless other factors that impact what being social will be like at your school. Every school is so different—the best way to get a good idea of what a specific school's social life will be like is to ask the students who go there. That being said, there are a few overarching myths about what being social in college is like, and, as per usual, we're here to bust them.

MYTH 1

THERE ARE NO CLIQUES OR STEREOTYPICAL GROUPS IN COLLEGE—EVERYBODY IS FRIENDS WITH EVERYBODY ELSE

You probably won't encounter the type of high school cliques that have been popularized (and stereotyped) by the media. If you're in the band, for instance, it doesn't make you a "band geek" who just *can't* speak to the jocks. But the truth is, in college, people do tend to define themselves based on social groups, if for no other reason than as a matter of practicality. These groups are composed of the people with whom you spend a lot of time (like the co-members of an extracurricular activity or the people on your hall) and, therefore, likely know the best. These groups aren't nefarious: Defining yourself in terms of group membership is essentially part of human nature, not to mention a perfectly acceptable and healthy way to bolster your identity.

These groups tend not to be rigid or exclusive, either. It's completely normal for stragglers to enter or interact with the group—people frequently bring along friends they know in other capacities to certain group-based parties. Being part of such groups hardly dictates your entire social experience, either—you're totally welcome and even expected to have other groups of friends outside of your main or specialized (extracurricular) group.

So, although depicting college as a love-fest in which everybody befriends everybody else is not terribly accurate, established groups do usually have fuzzy welcoming boundaries. If you encounter a group that is more like an exclusive, catty high school clique, chances are they're just jerks and are the exception rather than the rule. Some people just suck, no matter the greater social situation, and you will find them everywhere. But one of the best aspects of college is the *overall* open-minded norm of acceptance.

MYTH 2

POPULARITY DOESN'T EXIST IN COLLEGE

Like cliques, popularity can be a really aggressive phenomenon in high school. High school popularity is all about establishing a hierarchy of power by making some people feel subordinate and positioning some as clearly "better" than others. We never understood why some girls would rather be feared than loved and chose to take on what must have been an exhausting dedication to maintaining their status and calculating power plays. But then again, we're often told that we have old, world-weary souls, so that might explain that.

Popularity does exist in college, but it comes from a much more positive place: It's usually unilaterally about certain really outgoing, funny, or just plain likable people being well known and respected, not about making other people feel bad or positioning them as "lesser." Also, unlike high school, anybody can be popular within their own groups and in the greater campus social scene. Because there is no single, power-based hierarchy, generally, if you're a really cool person who has good relationships with a lot of other people, you meet a general standard for collegiate popularity.

MYTH 3

SOCIALIZING IS SUPER EASY IN COLLEGE— IT'S ONE BIG PARTY AND EVERYONE'S INVITED

Remember how in high school, you (or at least somebody you knew) always complained about how you always hung out with the same people every weekend and always did the same things? You can't wait to get to college, you profess; in college, there are a ton of different parties happening all the time, full of new and interesting people to meet. And that's definitely true— even at small schools, there are always opportunities to go out and meet new people. But once you get to college, you might start to crave the kind of regularity that often dictates the high school social experience.

Although social things *are* constantly happening on campus, and there are always people ready to go out and have a good time every night of the week, college isn't actually a love-fest in which everybody is included in everything—and that extends to partying. Just like you have to advocate for a great academic experience by constantly working on relationships with professors and staying on top of reading and assignments, you have to advocate for a great social experience by maintaining relationships with a wide group of friends and staying on top of what's going on in other people's lives and on campus. It's up to you to get your butt out there—to keep up relationships, to find out what's going on—as well as make good choices about when, where, and with whom you should be socializing in the first place. Ultimately, it's not *hard* to have a great, active social life: A ton of social opportunities are out there waiting for you. But you *do* have to try and, beyond that, make smart decisions.

IT'S OUR PARTY, WE CAN DO WHAT WE WANT... WITHIN REASON

We can't advocate partying in a guide to college for freshmen women, primarily because that would technically be advocating illegal activity (which we WOULD NEVER DO), but what we can suggest is to educate yourself about what partying at college is like—how to have (responsible) fun, stay safe, and make good choices (looks like our maternal instincts are kicking in). And here's how.

TO DRINK OR NOT TO DRINK?

If you don't drink at a college party, there is a universal understanding that everybody will crowd around you and torment you. They'll shout horrible obscenities at you and voice your deepest insecurities for hours until they eventually throw you into a pool/pile of garbage/whatever else is on hand. They will then douse you in Franzia, Natty Light, or another stereotypical college-geared alcoholic(ish) beverage available in large supply to torment you about your decision.

Just kidding. If you don't want to drink, nobody cares. You might get some lighthearted crap about it for like five seconds—maybe a little longer if it's a guy who is trying to chat you up, and perhaps a little longer than that if he's already quite intoxicated. And if anybody does have a problem with the fact that you're not drinking, rest assured that it's because they're insecure or self-conscious about their own drinking practices and want some kind of validation about it—and that's on them, not you.

There are plenty of reasons why people choose not to drink at college parties, and plenty of people make that choice. In fact, about 28% of college students don't drink at all—a growth of 8% over the last two decades (O'Connell-Domenech 2023).

But just a fair warning: Being a sober person at a party full of drunk people is usually not a great time. Although it's truly the best opportunity to observe humanity at its worst, unless you have a sober buddy with whom you can make fun of everybody else, you may just want to explore totally sober social options (which can be great and definitely more intellectually stimulating). Then again, there's always the often thankless but necessary role of designated driver (or, in the city, designated walkers and/or cab hailers). No matter what path you choose, it's totally possible to be sober *and* social—and, really, just miss out on some regrettable decisions and horrible hangovers.

The fact remains, though: Drinking happens at college. Just like every other aspect of college, there will be many varied opportunities to consume alcohol, and how you engage is up to you. But it's important to be aware of the reality that women approach drinking from a specific vantage point and are influenced by many factors that men may not be, including:

◇ **Body image issues:** "Drunkorexia" is a phenomenon in which predominantly young women starve themselves to offset the calories in alcoholic drinks they plan to consume and/or to get drunker faster. This practice is often an extension of an eating disorder, and, in fact, up to 50% of individuals with eating disorders use alcohol or illicit drugs, a rate five times higher than the general population (National Eating Disorder Association 2017).

◇ **Abuse:** Binge drinking is often a coping mechanism for traumas that disproportionately affect women. One study found that women who had experienced physical and sexual abuse were over six times more likely to be heavy drinkers (Skinner, Kristman-Valente, and Herrenkohl 2015).

◊ **Mental health issues:** Drinking is a widely employed coping mechanism for mental health issues, and research shows that women are more likely to use alcohol to cope with stress, depression, and anxiety (Barbosa et al. 2022).

For these reasons and more (like lack of self-esteem, specific peer pressure especially associated with sororities, the list goes on), college-aged women approach drinking in a different way than men. And yet, we're encouraged to approach it the same way: Enter "bro culture" (also known as "frat culture"), which is basically defined by drinking and is increasingly informing how the women who drink do so.

Admittedly, drinking has always been a stereotypical cornerstone of the college experience (see *Animal House, National Lampoon*, etc.). But whereas it was previously a male-dominated phenomenon, that's no longer the case. This is our version of equality: Collegiate women are expected to drink and party as much as their male friends can, despite women's hormonal and metabolic differences that decrease our tolerance for alcohol compared to men.

Even within this prevailing bro culture, it's possible to advocate for yourself and make your own (safe) choices. It's always possible to find parties that are a little tamer and aren't based on this type of behavior. If you do go to parties like this and feel others are peer pressuring you into drinking or doing anything else you're uncomfortable with, then *leave*: They clearly aren't people worth being around. If it's specifically guys who are pressuring you to drink, and if they're doing so in a way that leads you to believe they're trying to gain control over you, then the best option is to remove yourself from the environment immediately.

PARTY SAFETY TIPS

- *Always* **go out and stick with friends:** The buddy system was not just designed for frazzled preschool teachers to keep track of their students' tendencies to wander—it should be a nonnegotiable rule for going out. If you choose to go out with people you don't know or if you're on a date with someone new, let a close friend or roommate know where you are and try to check in periodically. Better safe than sorry.
- **Watch your drunk friends like a hawk:** At least 50% of student sexual assaults involve alcohol (Editorial Staff 2022). Being the victim of rape is never the victim's fault, but it's still important to watch out for your friends. Also, anybody intoxicated should never attempt to walk or drive home alone or go off with people they don't know. Do drunk friends a solid and make sure you stick together.
- **Know the signs of alcohol poisoning:** If your friend or anybody else you know starts to vomit, has seizures, is breathing really slowly (fewer than eight breaths per minute) or irregularly (two seconds or more between breaths), or is displaying signs of mental confusion (if they're in a stupor or cannot be roused) or hypothermia (low body temperature, bluish or extremely pale skin color), then she probably has alcohol poisoning. These signs indicate that somebody has ingested a potentially fatal dose of alcohol, and if you have any suspicions that she has, call 911 immediately. Seriously, even if you don't know this person, even if you're not 100% sure, and, yes, even if she is obviously under 21 and you're afraid that she could get in trouble, you could save a life.
- **Be safe on campus:** Lock your door—always, as a general rule, but especially if there's a party in the general vicinity. Besides the fact that being woken up at three a.m. by some drunk random who thinks you're her roommate and who won't shut up about "that jerk Freddy" is a pain in the butt, it's just a good idea because she could be the least of your worries. Program campus safety's number into your phone and even put it on speed dial (if you're calling campus safety, you'll probably be too panicked to look the number up). Also, some campuses offer self-defense classes—it might seem like overkill, but while you'll hopefully never need those skills, you might be glad you have them.

Basically, drinking happens at college in ways tame, dangerous, and everything in between. It's worth reiterating that drinking as a college freshman is illegal, but we all know it happens and that you will be presented with plenty of opportunities to drink and engage in other illegal activities. There is no prescription for how to deal with these situations: The only hard and fast rules we can offer (in addition to the party safety tips we just went over) are that you should know and respect your limits, only do things with which you feel completely comfortable, and make sure there are people you know and trust with you and watching out for you at all times. As with most things in life, the best way to prepare for the unknown is to really, truly know yourself: If you do, you'll be able to handle anything thrown at you.

NETFLIX IS NOT AN EXTRACURRICULAR: HOW TO GET INVOLVED

In college, nobody will drag you away from bingeing your favorite show for the thousandth time and *demand* that you get off your lazy ass and join a campus club or organization. Like everything else in college, your dedication, your involvement, basically your every action is totally on you.

Maybe after years of two-a-day sports practices or a scarring experience with a truly deranged speech and debate coach, you just feel like you're done. You've put in your extracurricular time, and besides, what's even in it for you anymore? You got into school and have to wonder if a future employer in the field of financial consulting/advertising/graphic design is going to care if you were the treasurer of the culinary society. What's the point?

Although the main point of extracurricular activities in high school may have been to demonstrate leadership ability, dedication, or specific skills to a college admissions officer (and, hopefully, was rewarding in some authentic way), getting involved in campus organizations serves a different purpose in college. It's something you should do for *yourself.* Joining or even leading a club, becoming a part of a supportive group that encourages you to explore an untapped passion, skill, or ability, is about investing in your own personal fulfillment, development, and happiness. Whether it's a group based on academics, athletics, cultural interest, philanthropy, or beyond, extracurricular activities can actually be so much more than résumé builders: They can impact your life in authentic and rewarding ways. Skeptical? Well, here's how.

THEY TEACH YOU ABOUT YOURSELF

Here's a secret about extracurriculars most kids aren't clued in on in high school: They don't have to be annoying time-suckers. In high school, so many kids pick their extracurriculars based on their potential to bolster their college résumés. For example, they'd join the "Environmental Club" not because they were concerned about climate change but because hardly anybody else was in it, and they knew they could easily take on a role like "Vice President" that looked good on paper. Hence, our grandchildren will only ever hear about mythical creatures called polar bears, but that's another matter entirely.

But joining a group can be incredibly fulfilling and impart valuable lessons about yourself as you explore potential interests. Women often struggle with taking risks: We tend to only get involved in things we know we can excel at and avoid new things because we fear failure. If we shed that fear and go after what we want or what we think we *might* want to try—even if that means putting ourselves in a position of vulnerability and accepting we might not be great at it—we're more likely to learn something new about ourselves. After all, nobody has ever learned anything valuable about herself or grown as a person by playing it safe.

THEY PROMOTE LEADERSHIP

The most compelling reason to get involved in something should probably be because you love it, not so that you can plot your way to world domination. That said, access to a leadership opportunity is actually a vital aspect of extracurricular involvement—and something, as women, we need to be vigilant about and continue to pursue.

The statistics are out there: Women are disgustingly underrepresented at the top levels of most major professional fields. Of the 2023 Fortune 500 CEO positions, only 10.4% were women (Hinchliffe 2023). Women composed 28% of the seats in the 118th U.S. Congress (Rutgers Center for American Women and Politics 2023). The percentage of women in tech leadership roles has fallen to 28% (Neal et al. 2023).

There are a lot of opinions out there as to *why* women are underrepresented in leadership positions, including structural barriers (White men tend to hire and promote people who look and act just like them) and women's socialization (a fear of appearing too ambitious if we try to network or self-promote, as well as work–life balance concerns that don't seem to affect or distract our male partners in the same way). But, ultimately, pursuing and having experience with leadership through extracurriculars as early as high school and continuing through college will only better prepare us to successfully pursue leadership positions in the future.

THEY PROVIDE YOU WITH A NETWORK OF LIKE-MINDED PEERS AND A SENSE OF GROUP IDENTITY

Ask any current college students how they met their friends or significant other; more often than not, they'll tell you that they forged their most valued relationships through mutual nonacademic involvement. Getting involved in some formal activity or group is the best way to meet like-minded peers, and it's hard to quantify the many benefits of surrounding yourself with people with whom you feel at home. You could meet someone who encourages you to take up a hobby you never thought to pursue (and end up being awesome at) or somebody you connect with on a deeper level.

In high school, many of us had two types of friends: those with whom we grew up and had known forever and those who we met through extracurriculars and shared values or identity. It's the same type of thing in college: You'll make friends based on location (usually, people from your freshman year dorm), with whom you bond because they're nice, sure, but mostly because they're there and available. And then you'll make friends because you genuinely have something in common—a fellow aspiring journalist you meet through the campus newspaper or somebody who shares your passion for social justice you meet through your campus's Amnesty International chapter.

The friendships made from the latter source tend to transcend time and distance. It's those people who have pushed and shaped Julie and Anna in important and lasting ways.

Especially at the beginning of the year, clubs and organizations will be in recruitment mode, breaking out everything from free candy to freewheeling compliments to entice you to join them. You have the advantage here: These groups need new members for obvious reasons (to replace graduating seniors, to reinvigorate the organization, to feast on nubile freshman blood, etc.). Take advantage of their recruiting impulse. Although these groups will undoubtedly be ready to spoon-feed you an idealized pitch about their organization, make sure you get the real information—the time commitment, leadership opportunities, or other advantages (like internship opportunities).

THE TRUTH ABOUT GOING GREEK

In high school, many of us have a very specific idea about what Greek life is like thanks to media in which frat boys homoerotically get drunk together and then objectify women and in which sorority sisters are vapid, hierarchical mean girls. Julie watched those movies and saw no room for herself within what frankly appeared to be an antiquated excuse for being a crappy human. She didn't feel any burning desire to find her long-lost nongenetic "sisters" or to participate in creepy rituals.

And yet, Julie found living away from home for the first time in a giant city challenging. She made good friends her first semester of freshman year but never bonded in that closer way: She didn't feel like they were shoulders to cry on or that she could have any kind of real talk with them. She craved the closeness she had with her high school best friends, whom she considered sisters. For that reason, she tried to keep an open mind as she enrolled in formal recruitment at the beginning of her second semester of freshman year.

It ended up being a good decision. Feeling like she belonged somewhere—among a diverse group of amazing and accomplished women, no less—was incredibly comforting. It was also surprising to Julie since, in high school, she would've laughed in your face had you told her she'd one day be in a sorority.

That being said, although, according to a recent Gallup Poll, there are an estimated 750,000 fraternity and sorority members in college and more than nine million alumni in the United States, Greek life is not for everybody (Barshay 2021). The experience varies widely from school to school and even from particular sorority chapter to chapter. It's also a true commitment—in terms of time, energy, and (notoriously) money, so weigh the following pros and cons and keep an open mind before making a decision.

THE PROS OF GREEK LIFE

- **The sense of community:** The downside of the overwhelming independence that's part and parcel of the college experience is how easy it is to get caught up in your routine and responsibilities and feel disconnected from something bigger. Being part of an inherently tight-knit group on campus can give you a strong sense of belonging.
- **Easy and always-available friendship:** Before Julie joined a sorority, the idea that dozens of girls would just be willing to be friends with her based on a common group membership alone seemed a little shallow and disingenuous. It wasn't until she actually experienced having a virtual stranger open her arms and accept the possibility of friendship without a second thought that she realized there was nothing fake about it—that the world would be a much better place if we treated everybody like potential friends rather than a weirdo until proven worthy.
- **Philanthropy work:** A significant part of being in a sorority is raising money and holding events for and facilitating a partnership with a philanthropic organization. We're all busy, but going Greek means committing to giving back in some way—and there's no downside to that.
- **Social opportunities:** There's always an opportunity to be social when you're Greek. Whether it's a mixer with a fraternity, a sisterhood bonding event, or even just the ability to call up any of your sisters on a whim to hang out, being part of a sorority basically guarantees you'll never be alone on a Saturday night. Unless, of course, a movie and a pint of ice cream are calling your name, but then again, there's always a sister more than willing to join you for that, too.
- **Academic standards:** All sororities require that you maintain a minimum GPA to remain in "good academic standing" (and therefore a part of the organization). If you're somebody who needs some external motivation to keep your

grades up, knowing that there are direct consequences for failing could be helpful.

♦ **Networking:** Meeting an alumna of your sorority outside of your college's Greek system is an awesome experience: You immediately feel a bond, and there's just an understanding that you will help each other out. This especially goes a long way when it comes to professional opportunities. Alumnae constantly reach out to their sorority at large as well as their specific chapters to offer internship or job opportunities and are always willing to hear from or help out a sister. Additionally, when it comes to your résumé, most employers understand the kind of responsibility and commitment holding a position within your Greek organization takes. They won't write you off for being in a sorority—they'll probably be impressed, especially if you took on a leadership role.

♦ **Housing:** Depending on where you go to school, the availability of Greek housing could be a pretty big deal. At some of the bigger universities, these homes can be *really* nice and include things like personal chefs and other services. However, at others, they're really not a big deal—it depends on your specific chapter and university.

THE CONS OF GOING GREEK

♦ **The financial commitment:** Yes, being in a sorority costs money; you have to pay dues, which can vary depending on which sorority you join as well as your specific chapter. However, most sororities have scholarships and other financial aid opportunities and are willing to work with anyone who demonstrates financial need.

♦ **The time commitment:** Between recruitment, chapter (a mandatory weekly meeting for the entire sorority), committee meetings, social events, and other sorority gatherings, going Greek is no small time commitment. It can easily consume your entire life if you let it, and many girls like it for that very reason—they want to be consumed by something bigger than themselves, surrounded by their friends at all times. But if you do have other passions and commitments, it's something to consider. You especially want to make sure you have enough time for class and studying.

♦ **When it comes first (and shouldn't):** Some sorority girls take their Greek identity way too seriously. Whether it's forcing their sisters to stay up until three a.m. baking all of the cupcakes for some fundraiser or just generally making themselves martyrs to the sorority experience, there are always going to be girls who didn't get the memo that being part of a sorority should *supplement* the other aspects of your life, especially your academic commitments. In fact, it's a serious red flag if you ever feel pressured by your sorority to skip class or not study as much as you should to prove your "loyalty" to your sisters.

♦ **Emphasis on partying:** Just like Greek life in general, partying should *supplement* the rest of your Greek experience—not define it. There's nothing wrong with joining an organization for the sake of letting loose and meeting new people. But if that becomes a nightly endeavor or begins to interfere with other more substantial aspects of your life, and if you feel you're developing unhealthy habits because of it, then it's time to reevaluate.

♦ **Questionable social practices:** There are some unfair stereotypes about Greek life, but there are also nuggets of truth to some of them. Recruiting in Greek organizations necessitates the ranking and judgment of other women, and that really uncool aspect of the process is nothing to sneeze at. It's also pretty undisputed that legacies and girls of certain economic profiles are unfairly favored above those who don't have those kinds of privileges, which is, to be blunt, bullshit.

Also, a word on hazing: If it happens, run away. Seriously. Hazing is never okay and is actually a form of domestic violence. There are a lot of great aspects of sororities that are often misunderstood, but elitism, discrimination, and hazing are downsides to the entire system (although they are by no means present in every chapter of every sorority). However, it's important to remain vigilant and never tolerate that kind of behavior if you encounter it.

ON CULTURAL AND MULTICULTURAL SORORITIES

Although sororities under the National Panhellenic Conference (the traditional Greek life organization) admit women from all socioeconomic backgrounds, they tend to be predominately Caucasian. Cultural sororities (which exclusively admit women of a specific culture) and multicultural sororities (which actively recruit women of diverse cultures) can be attractive options for many women.

Having an opportunity to create cultural unity and escape tokenism by surrounding yourself with people who share your cultural identity is especially salient, considering that studies show that higher education still has a diversity problem. In fact, one study found that at the current rate of change, it will still take about 70 years for higher education institutions to fully reflect underrepresented students in their student populations (Ellsworth et al. 2022). Cultural and multicultural Greek organizations offer a great community for students who may be wary of the lack of diversity surrounding them at large.

The National Pan-Hellenic Council, which was founded in 1930 and serves as a governing body for historically Black fraternities and sororities, is probably the most widely recognized (and historically established) of the many "cultural interest" organizations. Four of the nine organizations the Council governs are sororities: Alpha Kappa Alpha, Delta Sigma Theta, Zeta Phi Beta, and Sigma Gamma Rho. However, there are also Asian American (under the National APIA Panhellenic Association), Latina (under the National Association of Latino Fraternal Organizations), and generally multicultural (under the National Multicultural Greek Council) sororities as well. There are even religious-based sororities, including Jewish, Muslim, and Christian organizations, and groups based on other identities, like being LGBTQ+.

Basically, if you're at all interested in Greek life, a cultural or multicultural sorority may be the way to go. Beyond diversity, you could very well find that such a sorority exemplifies the type of leadership, character, and values (all qualities that should inform your decision to join any Greek organization) that specifically resonate best with you.

THE DIRTY ON DOING THE DIRTY: THE REAL DEAL ABOUT HOOKING UP

We can't talk about college without discussing sex and all the complex things that come with desire. Of course, it's often difficult to discuss what hooking up is *actually* like, not only because it's a very personal, individual, and varied experience but also because conversations around sex and what we do with our bodies often become incredibly moralistic.

Well, we're not here to judge or suggest that there's one "correct" or "normal" way to approach sex in college. But we can clear up a few misconceptions and offer you a little bit of advice based on our own mistakes, awkward moments, and joys.

THE MOST COMMON MISCONCEPTIONS ABOUT HOOKING UP

The week before college started, Anna was worried about a lot of things, including whether she would get along with her roommates, get lost on the way to class, and be invited to parties. But the number one thing she was worried about was whether or not she'd be the only virgin on campus.

Julie had a similar experience. After years of watching romantic comedies with horrible plots, cheesy dialogue, and middle-aged actors cast as teenage students, she assumed everyone in high school and college was having sex all the time. Before her freshman year, she worried everyone would smell the inexperience on her and shun her.

That ended up being just one of several of the biggest misconceptions about sex in college:

◊ **Everyone already has sexual experience:** While it might seem like everyone is having sex or has had sex, many college freshmen haven't. In fact, one survey found that 30% of teens reported having had sex (Centers for Disease Control and Prevention 2023a). The truth is that while some people may modify their sexual stories to avoid feeling embarrassed or to try to fit in, everyone arrives at college with a different level of sexual experience.

◊ **Everyone's hooking up all the time:** Even those who have had sex are hardly hooking up nonstop. Recent research finds that Americans between the ages of 18 and 23 are having significantly less casual sex than previous generations (South and Lei 2021).

◊ **Everyone's completely confident in their sexuality:** Some people come to college having known their sexual orientation their entire lives, while others need more time to figure out how they identify. There is no schedule you should be following or due date by which you need to figure it all out. Campus LGBTQIA+ groups can be a helpful resource for those exploring their sexuality since they are safe spaces to ask questions and find community.

Wanting to fit in is normal and understandable, but since the true "normal" may not be clear (or exist at all), it's best to have the sex you want to have and not the sex you think you should be having—if you want to have it at all.

Anna learned this the hard way: After getting out of a serious relationship in college, she was determined to figure out how to hook up without emotion. She wanted to be able to coolly say things like, "Oh yeah, that guy? We slept together. It was average. Never spoke again." And then go about her day.

To save you from getting too involved in her hero's journey, we'll cut to the chase: She failed. For her, and for many people, sex is vulnerable and it's difficult to untie the physical act from the emotional connection. That said, she only learned that by trying, and now has the following advice:

◊ **Make "mistakes":** We tend to look back on experiences that weren't the most pleasant or didn't precisely align with what we want for ourselves with shame. While this instinct is understandable, since our society tends to generally view sex through a lens of shame, it can be helpful to reframe these "mistakes" as opportunities to learn more about ourselves. Part of learning who you are sexually is figuring out what you like and don't like.

◊ **You're allowed to change your mind:** You might go through a period where you love casual sex and then one where you want a deeper connection with a partner. You might want romantic sex one night and rough sex another, and that's okay! It's normal to change your mind about what you want and change it back. Listen to your needs and try to communicate them with your partner.

◊ **You can care even when things are casual:** If the goal of sex is to connect and give one another pleasure, then care will, and should, be involved. To be attuned to your partner's needs, you need to be aware of how their body is responding—you need to care about their experience. If it seems like they want to slow down or take a break, listen to them, and they should do the same for you. You are allowed to have wants, desires, and needs, and if someone makes you feel bad for wanting those things, then simply put, they are not good in bed.

◊ What's more, you are allowed to care about your sexual partner—to like them or have a crush. You are allowed to want love. It seems like there's a lot of pressure to be able to hook up with someone and be totally chill about it the next day, and if you can roll with that, sick. If you are someone who can't, that's also fine.

◇ **If you feel like you're being mistreated, take that instinct seriously:** We delved into some of the darker parts of sex and relationships in Chapter 4, including dating violence and sexual assault, but it bears repeating: If you feel like something is wrong or are uncomfortable with a situation, listen to your instincts and value your judgment.

TO BREAK UP OR NOT TO BREAK UP? THAT IS THE QUESTION

It's the question every high school couple faces when they prepare to head off to different schools: Should we try long distance? Although you and your significant other are (obviously) the only people who truly understand your relationship, you'll find that *everybody* will have an opinion about its future. It's likely that your parents and friends will be wary about the prospect of you staying with your high school sweetheart, especially if you're going to different schools and *especially* if those schools are geographically distant.

"Why would you want to hold yourself back by staying with somebody from high school?" you'll inevitably be asked. "College is a time for exploration—for new experiences with new people," somebody will probably pat themselves on the back for pointing out to you.

These are all valid points, and there are many legitimate reasons to break up with your boyfriend or girlfriend when going off to college, including:

◇ **Physically holding yourself back:** Especially if you go to different schools, you might allocate free time you could've spent establishing your own life on your campus by visiting your significant other and getting to know his or her friends. There's nothing inherently wrong with this—you could certainly meet cool people at your boyfriend or girlfriend's school. But you deserve to have your own independent experience: You should embrace establishing your life beyond your significant other's. And, in case of a breakup, it's important to have a support system and other valuable people in your life. Letting your entire existence revolve around someone else is *never* a healthy choice.

◊ **Emotionally holding yourself back:** Establishing yourself at college your freshman year is difficult but necessary. It's the same process you'll undoubtedly have to repeat throughout your life every time you have a new job, move to a new place, or make new friends. Especially if you're introverted or shy, it's all too easy to rely on an already established relationship during this time, to use it as a crutch and keep yourself from engaging in the difficult but vitally important process of connecting with new people. It's also hard to grow as an individual if you're still trying to be the same person your significant other fell for in your teens. You owe it to yourself to find out everything you're capable of and the fully amazing person you can be.

◊ **Holding yourself back from other informative relationships:** One of the amazing things about college is that people with different life experiences and points of view surround you. You may feel that you and your significant other belong together because you're so similar...overlooking what a relationship with somebody completely different from you could teach you. You shouldn't necessarily break up with your high school boyfriend or girlfriend to embark on a quest to find your *real* soulmate (although that's a possibility), but rather to embrace exploration and find out what you want and need from a relationship (and what you don't) by embracing the possibility of failed relationships with unlikely partners.

But, again, at the end of the day, only you can gauge what your relationship truly means to you and if staying together is the best option. The go-to, strong, independent lady advice may be to break up and forge your own identity, but while no woman *needs* a partner, having a significant other can be a positive and empowering experience, and there's a lot to be said for sticking with a relationship with someone you love.

If you decide to stay in a high school relationship in college, however, there are some new things you should be vigilant about that you may not have previously considered.

◊ **It's all about trust:** To maintain a healthy relationship while also establishing your identity and life on your own campus, you need to establish boundaries with your significant other and then trust them. For your relationship to work, you need to trust that the person your significant other is hugging in their Instagram story is just a friend. You need to trust that they are telling the truth about their plans for the night and refrain from texting them or their friends demanding to know their whereabouts (and if you're on the receiving end of such behavior, put an end to it immediately). You also need to trust yourself. If you feel that you can't be around others without worrying about how it might look or how you feel about it, then that's a serious warning sign that your relationship may not be stable enough to survive long distance.

◇ **Communication is key:** Although you shouldn't be giving your partner a daily itinerary of your activities and checking in with them every five minutes (unhealthy behavior alert!), you should be open and honest about what you're doing and who you're hanging out with. If you feel like you want to or need to hide something, like a new friendship, it's a serious red flag. And if you *do* meet somebody else you have confusing (or pretty clear) romantic feelings for, don't hide it. It might seem like you're trying to hurt your partner by telling them you like somebody else, but you're doing the best thing for both of you by being honest and assessing where you're at before you *really* hurt them by cheating.

◇ **Check in with yourself:** You'll need to be incredibly open and honest with yourself about how you feel about your relationship in a way you may not have in high school. Accept that you and your significant other might grow apart and that things between you two will inevitably change due to a lack of time together and distance.

There's nothing wrong with trying to make a relationship work if you think it's worth it, but also make sure you're not disillusioned about it. Being honest with yourself is usually deceptively harder than being honest with your partner; it's easy to convince yourself to stay in a relationship that feels so comfortable and with somebody you have a history with, but it's important to stay true to yourself.

Also, never stay with somebody only because you don't think anyone else will like you—that is untrue and an unfair and unhealthy reason to stay in any relationship, long-distance or not.

I'LL BE THERE FOR YOU... IF YOU'RE THERE FOR ME, TOO: MAKING (AND LOSING) FRIENDS

MAKING NEW FRIENDS: HOW TO FIND YOUR PLATONIC SOULMATE

In high school, Julie had five best friends who did everything together and knew the intimate details of each other's lives. However, like many friend groups, they all ended up at different colleges. Although she was thankful for having deep friendships, those connections also led her to struggle to make friends during the beginning of her freshman year.

She didn't necessarily have a problem meeting people: There was her new roommate, the many girls on her hall, and the countless students she met at the many orientation week activities. What she found so difficult was wading through the annoying (yet necessary) shallow conversations that constantly followed the same pattern: name, hometown, expected major, reason for choosing this school, etc.

Even beyond her group of best friends, Julie went to the same tiny school her whole life, largely alongside the same people she had known since preschool. After almost exclusively socializing with people she had known since childhood, it was frustrating to have to start from scratch. *Will I ever find anybody who I connect with and who understands me like my high school friends?* she wondered on a daily basis. *How do people make new friends again?*

Ultimately, she was not fated for the life of a recluse—she did end up making friends. But those relationships didn't happen without effort, without constantly putting herself out there and pushing herself way past her (introverted) comfort zone.

Of course, struggling the way Julie did is not the universal freshman experience. One of her best friends from high school immediately bonded with the girls on her hall in the first week of school. Another rushed a sorority her first semester and became completely integrated into that community. They all found their people one way or another eventually. There is no formula for making new friends, but there are a few steps you can take to ensure you'll at least meet new people with whom you'll hopefully bond.

◇ **Join extracurricular activities:** As mentioned in the section on extracurriculars, most people meet their best friends and the people with whom they most authentically connect through a group based on a shared interest or passion. Especially during your first semester, attend a few different clubs' meetings to get a sense of where you think you'll fit in and can be a valuable part of the group. Try to meet as many people as possible, and don't be afraid to ask people if they want to meet up outside of the group. Get used to asking people out on friend dates.

◇ **Consider Greek life:** Greek life is based on the benefits of being part of a strong community. Once you're in a sorority, you can basically approach any other member, and they will be friendly and completely open to getting to know you better. There are few other venues in life that are this amenable to creating friendships with a completely open mind. Even if you don't ultimately rush a sorority or feel like you want to drop out down the line, the recruitment process alone is a great way to meet a ton of new people—sisters and fellow potential new members alike.

◇ **Get to know your roommate/hallmates:** This is probably the easiest option. For at least the first few weeks of school, you should always keep your door open (except for when, you know, you need some alone time or are unconscious). It invites people to stop by and chat. Likewise, if somebody else has their door open, you should stop by and introduce yourself. Hopefully, you'll also have a really enthusiastic and dedicated RA who does their best to facilitate hall activities that allow you to get to know everybody else a little better.

◊ **Be extroverted:** It can be hard to put yourself out there and go out of your way to get to know complete strangers. But doing so is part and parcel of the freshman experience. If you're naturally extroverted, this is your time to shine. If you're introverted, do your best impression of an extrovert. If you don't overthink it, it totally works.

OUT OF THE MOUTHS OF ~~BABES~~ CURRENT COLLEGE STUDENTS

Making New Friends in College

When I started college, I tried to meet as many people as I could. It's important not to have any preconceived notions about who your best friends will be for the next few years because college offers the chance to meet a lot of interesting people. You'll form distinct groups of friends from your history class, dorm, and even internships. There were so many remarkable people I met, but building a strong friendship takes time and energy. I discovered that it's impossible to become close to everyone, but by actively reaching out for lunch or checking in with people, you can maintain a great network of people.

—Celeste, Stamford University

LOSING OLD FRIENDS: HOW HIGH SCHOOL FRIENDSHIPS CHANGE

It's an inevitable consequence of time and distance: Your friendships with high school friends *will* change, generally as a matter of practicality: You're embedded in different cultures, surrounded by different people and other influential factors, and will all change in ways that create an unprecedented gap.

You don't necessarily have to lose these friendships altogether, though—there are ways to stay in touch and keep those friendships alive:

◊ **Set up a regular, nonnegotiable time to talk:** College students are all constantly busy, but if you want to maintain a friendship, it's essential to keep in touch beyond a text here or there. Find a time on a regular basis when you and your best friend or group of best friends can get on FaceTime and see each other's' faces, hear each other's' voices, and connect in a way that is facilitated but not defined or restricted by technology.

◊ **Actually catch them up on life events:** Even if you're dealing with complicated feelings or detailed situations specific to your group of college friends, fill your high school friends in. It's easy to unintentionally forget to tell these friends about significant things that happen in your life, but that can make them feel like you purposely kept something important from them. If you want to prevent your friendship from becoming superficial, you have to *really* keep your friends up to date.

◊ **Cut them some slack:** Your friends are going to change throughout college. So will you. And none of you can take it personally. Try not to judge them for any actions that seem out of character, but rather try to understand that they're dealing with new situations and people and are trying to find their place in it all. If you're in a friendship for the long haul, you need to be willing to make it through some bumps in the road.

Being social in college may be as valuable an experience as any class you take or content you learn—but only in a balanced way. Partying every night isn't going to help you grow as a person, but testing your limits, making valuable and real connections with a diverse array of people, and tapping into new passions and talents offer one of the most meaningful experiences of growth you'll find in your (semi) adult life. These social experiences will allow you to evolve the most as an individual, and that will shape the adult you'll eventually become—not memorizing the process of mitosis or the intricate tenets of Karl Marx's view of production.

So, although the academic aspect of your college education is important for very predictable reasons—for the content you will learn, for the GPA you'll earn that will lead to graduate schools, and the degree that will lead to employment—the social aspect of college is equally as important for unpredictable reasons. The social aspects of college will likely bring the big, blurry question mark of who you are and your purpose in life into focus, and that's definitely an experience you don't want to miss out on.

REFERENCES

Barbosa, Carolina, William N. Dowd, Alan Barnosky, and Katherine J. Karriker-Jaffe. 2022. "Alcohol Consumption During the First Year of the COVID-19 Pandemic in the United States: Results from a Nationally Representative Longitudinal Survey." *Journal of Addiction Medicine*, July. https://doi.org/10.1097/adm.0000000000001018.

Barshay, Jill. 2021. "PROOF POINTS: New Poll Points to College and Career Benefits of Greek Life Despite Criticism." The Hechinger Report. July 19. https://hechingerreport.org/proof-points-new-poll-points-to-college-and-career-benefits-of-greek-life-despite-criticism/.

Centers for Disease Control and Prevention. 2023a. "Sexual Risk Behaviors." March 16. https://www.cdc.gov/healthyyouth/sexualbehaviors/index.htm.

Editorial Staff. 2022. "Sexual Assaults on College Campuses Involving Alcohol." American Addiction Centers. October 25. https://alcohol.org/health-effects/sexual-assault-college-campus/.

Ellsworth, Diana, Erin Harding, Jonathan Law, and Duwain Pinder. 2022. "Racial and Ethnic Equity in US Higher Education." McKinsey & Company. July 18. www.mckinsey.com/industries/education/our-insights/racial-and-ethnic-equity-in-us-higher-education.

Hinchliffe, Emma. 2023. "Women CEOs Run 10.4% of Fortune 500 Companies. A Quarter of the 52 Leaders Became CEO in the Last Year." Fortune. June 5. https://fortune.com/2023/06/05/fortune-500-companies-2023-women-10-percent/.

National Eating Disorder Association. 2017. "Substance Use and Eating Disorders." National Eating Disorders Association. October 5. www.nationaleatingdisorders.org/substance-use-and-eating-disorders.

Neal, Stephanie, Rosey Rhyne, Jazmine Boatman, Bruce Watt, and Mindy Yeh. 2023. "Global Leadership Forecast 2023." DDI World. www.ddiworld.com/global-leadership-forecast-2023.

O'Connell-Domenech, Alejandra. 2023. "Why Is Gen Z Drinking Less?" The Hill. April 6. https://thehill.com/changing-america/well-being/3936579-why-is-gen-z-drinking-less/.

Rutgers Center for American Women and Politics. 2023. "Women in Elective Office 2023." Rutgers University. https://cawp.rutg ers.edu/facts/current-numbers/women-elective-office-2023.

Skinner, Martie L., Allison N. Kristman-Valente, and Todd I. Herrenkohl. 2015. "Adult Binge Drinking: Childhood Sexual Abuse, Gender and the Role of Adolescent Alcohol-Related Experiences." *Alcohol and Alcoholism* 51(2): 136–141. https:// doi.org/10.1093/alcalc/agv093.

South, Scott J., and Lei Lei. 2021. "Why Are Fewer Young Adults Having Casual Sex?" *Socius: Sociological Research for a Dynamic World*, March. https://doi.org/10.1177/2378023121996854.

CHAPTER 7

HOW TO DO COLLEGE

(or Why All of This Matters)

There is no bullet-point list of How to Do College. There is no foolproof, detailed list of steps to take and things to accomplish before you graduate. We might perpetuate the idea that it's possible to have a "perfect" college experience that will transform you into an ideal version of yourself, superiorly prepared to face adulthood, but the truth is there are as many college experiences as there are humans who go to college: There is no perfect college experience—or any other type of perfect experience for that matter (and we don't think anybody is ever prepared to face adulthood, but that's a whole other thing).

At the end of the day, there are only individuals who have personal experiences based on how they choose to approach the novel situations with which they're presented. On levels both intimately singular and collective as women, we need to let go of this idealistic portrayal of college and embrace the far more nuanced and dynamic reality.

 DOI: 10.4324/9781003408932-7

But accepting that this idealistic portrayal is false hardly necessitates accepting defeat: It's *more* than possible to have an incredible college experience. Sentimental and sappy though it may sound, you probably *will* meet lifelong friends with whom you'll make countless lasting memories. You'll attend classes and interact with professors who will change the way you view and experience the world around you. You'll get involved in a club or activity that will help you discover a dormant passion or ability. You will have a number of other life-altering experiences that we couldn't begin to guess at or describe.

Reading this book will give you a leg up toward achieving these things, it's true—where else can you find honest information about hooking up that doesn't present young women as one-dimensional caricatures, advice on how to avoid social leper status, and guidance on how to best navigate paying for school to avoid turning into a bitter conspiracy theorist?

But ultimately, being a passive consumer of this information isn't going to cut it. There are still three major things you have to actually *do* to have a truly great college experience.

TO DO #1

DISCARD PERFECTION

Young women often view the college experience as another step in their quest for perfection. We enter with insurmountable expectations of having an idyllic, sister-like relationship with our roommate, meeting a simultaneously intellectually stimulating yet romantic and compassionate partner, and finding an intellectual passion that will reveal a fulfilling life path. We envision a perfect experience because that's the standard to which young women are generally held in this society: The prospect of anything less is a failure because there is no intermediary alternative. Thus, even while immersed in a college experience that, as we've tried to describe, hardly matches this perfected vision, we don't assume that society has failed *us* in its unrealistic depiction of college and that the college experience itself is actually much more complex than we expected. Rather, we conclude that *we* failed society in our personal inability to have the perfect college experience, and it's somehow our fault. We struggle alone to create an experience that doesn't exist instead of banding together to embrace the one that does.

We wish we had a prescription to cure perfectionism—that we could draw up another nifty diagram or neat bullet-point list to go along with all the rest in this book. But the truth is, we're hardly ones to preach about it.

Perfectionism dominated Julie's high school career and hardly abated her freshman year of college. The deeply held conception that she had to be the *best* at any cost dictated every feeling she had about and action she took surrounding her mind, body, and worth. She ended her freshman year with a near-perfect transcript but as a shell of herself.

It wasn't until Anna's senior year of college that she realized she had divorced herself from what she *actually* wanted to accomplish by letting her perfectionist anxiety be her main motivation. She looked at her grades, extracurriculars, and friends and realized that, as cheesy as it sounds, she had completely lost herself.

Both Julie and Anna eventually saw the disconnect between believing women should be able to have the lives they want while personally feeling defeated and empty. They finally decided to exchange striving for perfection for striving for what they really *wanted*—a distinction they previously hadn't even been aware existed. It took them a while to realize that striving for perfection didn't equate to happiness but had only ever inspired the opposite.

The truth is, though, overcoming perfectionism isn't easy: It's about continuously making deliberate choices. It's about purposefully ignoring what we think we should do, be, or look like. It's about deciding not to even try to have it all but to try to have what we want and need. And to do that, we have to be willing to put it all on the line and embrace the risk of failure.

TO DO #2

WHOLEHEARTEDLY EMBRACE RISK-TAKING

Numerous studies suggest that women are less likely than men to take risks and go after what we want. This is not because women are biologically wired to be codependent, rule-following minions. In fact, research suggests women may avoid taking risks more than men because risks don't always pay off for women in the same way—women experience more negative consequences when they take risks, which dissuades them from doing so again (Morgenroth, Ryan, and Fine 2022). Basically, sexism keeps us from taking risks.

Taking risks also means opening ourselves up to the possibility of something we've been taught to avoid at all costs: failure. Considering young women are socialized to view failure as the complete antithesis of their very identities, it's no wonder we're incredibly reluctant to risk experiencing it. Therefore, we avoid risk altogether—we avoid the experiences and opportunities that could potentially inform and shape us into interesting, whole, and fulfilled human beings.

But, at the same time, college is an incredible opportunity to overcome this gender-specific ethos: It's probably the best chance we'll ever get to take the types of risks that will allow us to claim our own definitions of happiness and success and to finally go after them. In college, we have enough autonomy to thoughtfully and purposefully experiment—intellectually, emotionally, sexually, and beyond—but are still somewhat removed from having to make crucial, informative decisions that will directly impact the courses our lives will take. Now is the time to fearlessly figure out and pursue what we *really* want instead of going along with what we feel is expected of us. Only by taking control of our lives before we're inculcated by adult responsibilities do we have a shot in hell at the kind of happiness and satisfaction that can only be born from truly knowing ourselves and what we want.

This is certainly easier said than done, but we have to try—for not only ourselves but also the sake of all women.

TO DO #3

BE TRANSPARENT AND OPEN TO OTHERS

It's not enough to discard perfection and take risks: It's vital to be transparent about our decision to actively attempt both. Women need to be far more honest about the pressures we feel—from academics, to the difficulty of finding and maintaining friendships and relationships, to how we treat our bodies, and beyond. Collegiate women feel like they're struggling or failing largely because they buy into the façade *other* women enforce: that other women don't feel these pressures and that all failure—perceived or experienced—reflects who we *are* rather than something we've done.

Bottom line: We all feel defeated by life at some point or another, and we can break this cycle of internally struggling while externally projecting effortless success—which reinforces this perception of any struggle as a personal failure—by actively deciding to break it. We need to be completely upfront about the pressures we face and what we're doing to combat them and acknowledge when we take risks to erase the stigma of failing. Being open about these experiences with other women will not only make them feel better or encourage them to do the same but also cyclically help us by making this mentality the norm. By the same token, it's vital that we not only do this ourselves and encourage other women to do this but that we're also ready to accept them if and when they do.

Popular culture largely depicts college as an experience that leads to quantitative gains: as one in which an absurd number of parties are attended, friends are made, grades are earned, and a certain starting salary is expected. But ultimately, the best college experiences are *qualitatively* successful. College is an opportunity to put in motion the life you want—ideally, a happy one. It's not about what you've tangibly gained but about who you are at the other end.

The true beauty of college is that it's a period of your life that will truly be like nothing else you have experienced or will experience. What all of the wistful adults in your life say is true: It goes by *so* fast. Embrace it and live every day of it to the fullest because, even with this advice, there's no perfect or ideal way to experience college. You can prepare for the highs and lows, but at the end of the day, you just need to get out there and do it.

And, remember, you're a smart girl. All you need is a little fearlessness, self-forgiveness, and acceptance (and caffeine and chocolate), and you'll be fine.

REFERENCE

Morgenroth, Thekla, Michelle K. Ryan, and Cordelia Fine. 2022. "The Gendered Consequences of Risk-Taking at Work: Are Women Averse to Risk or to Poor Consequences?" *Psychology of Women Quarterly* 46(3). https://doi.org/10.1177/0361684322 1084048.

ABOUT THE AUTHORS

JULIE ZEILINGER

Julie Zeilinger is a writer and editor who has been named one of the "Forbes 30 Under 30," one of *Newsweek*'s "150 Women Who Shake the World," and one of the *Times of London*'s "40 Bloggers Who Really Count." She is the founder and editor of WMC FBomb, a feminist media platform for teens and young adults, partnered with Gloria Steinem, Jane Fonda, and Robin Morgan's organization, the Women's Media Center.

Julie has managed content for organizations including Girls Who Code and Supermajority, edited for MTV News and Vox, and her writing has been published in *Marie Claire, Vox, HuffPost, Forbes*, and other publications. She is also the author of two books: *College 101: A Girl's Guide to Freshman Year* and *A Little F'd Up: Why Feminism Is Not a Dirty Word* (2012).

Julie holds a bachelor's degree from Barnard College and a master's degree from The New School.

Learn more at juliezeilinger.com.

ANNA KOPPELMAN

Anna Koppelman is a New York-based writer and comedian. At 15, she began publishing her writing on the excitement, heartbreak, and wonder of growing up in national outlets like MTV, the *Huffington Post*, and *Entertainment Weekly*. If you're looking for her, she's probably off somewhere laughing.

REFERENCES

"The 1 in 6 Statistic." n.d. Sexual Abuse & Assault of Boys & Men | Confidential Support for Men. https://1in6.org/statistic/.

Barbosa, Carolina, William N. Dowd, Alan Barnosky, and Katherine J. Karriker-Jaffe. 2022. "Alcohol Consumption During the First Year of the COVID-19 Pandemic in the United States: Results from a Nationally Representative Longitudinal Survey." *Journal of Addiction Medicine*, July. https://doi.org/10.1097/adm.0000000000001018.

Barshay, Jill. 2021. "PROOF POINTS: New Poll Points to College and Career Benefits of Greek Life Despite Criticism." The Hechinger Report. July 19. https://hechingerreport.org/proof-points-new-poll-points-to-college-and-career-benefits-of-greek-life-despite-criticism/.

"Be More than a Bystander." n.d. Ending Violence BC. https://endingviolence.org/bystander/.

Beaudry, Kayleigh M., Izabella A. Ludwa, Aysha M. Thomas, Wendy E. Ward, Bareket Falk, and Andrea R. Josse. 2019.

"First-Year University Is Associated With Greater Body Weight, Body Composition and Adverse Dietary Changes in Males Than Females." Edited by David Meyre. *PLOS ONE* 14(7). https://doi.org/10.1371/journal.pone.0218554.

Bowe, Kristen. 2023. "College Students and Depression." Mayo Clinic Health System. August 22. www.mayoclinichealthsystem.org/hometown-health/speaking-of-health/college-students-and-depression.

Brody, Debra, Laura Pratt, and Jeffery Hughes. 2018. "Prevalence of Depression Among Adults Aged 20 and Over: United States, 2013—2016." Centers for Disease Control and Prevention. www.cdc.gov/nchs/products/databriefs/db303.htm#print.

"Campus Sexual Violence: Statistics." n.d. RAINN. www.rainn.org/statistics/campus-sexual-violence.

Caporal, Jack. 2023. "Student Loan Debt Statistics in 2023." The Motley Fool. August 1. www.fool.com/research/student-loan-debt-statistics/.

Centers for Disease Control and Prevention. 2022a. "STD Facts—Human Papillomavirus (HPV)." April 12. www.cdc.gov/std/HPV/STDFact-HPV.htm.

Centers for Disease Control and Prevention. 2022b. "Alcohol Use and Your Health." April 14. www.cdc.gov/alcohol/fact-sheets/alcohol-use.htm.

Centers for Disease Control and Prevention. 2023a. "Sexual Risk Behaviors." March 16. https://www.cdc.gov/healthyyouth/sexualbehaviors/index.htm.

Centers for Disease Control and Prevention. 2023b. "Detailed STD Facts—Chlamydia." April 12. www.cdc.gov/std/chlamydia/stdfact-chlamydia-detailed.htm.

Cleveland Clinic. 2022. "Masturbation: Facts & Benefits." October 25. https://my.clevelandclinic.org/health/articles/24332-masturbation.

Cuellar Mejia, Marisol, Cesar Alesi Perez, Vicki Hsieh, and Hans Johnson. 2023. "Is College Worth It?" Public Policy Institute of California. March. www.ppic.org/publication/is-college-worth-it/.

Dold, Kristen, Jasmine Gomez, Ashley Mateo, and Ashley Martens. 2022. "3 Common Causes of Sudden, Unexplained Weight Gain, According to Doctors." Women's Health Magazine. Spring 22. www.womenshealthmag.com/health/a19992956/unexplained-weight-gain/.

Editorial Staff. 2022. "Sexual Assaults on College Campuses Involving Alcohol." American Addiction Centers. October 25. https://alcohol.org/health-effects/sexual-assault-college-campus/.

Ellsworth, Diana, Erin Harding, Jonathan Law, and Duwain Pinder. 2022. "Racial and Ethnic Equity in US Higher Education." McKinsey & Company. July 18. www.mckinsey.com/industries/education/our-insights/racial-and-ethnic-equity-in-us-higher-education.

Hanson, Melanie. 2021. "Average Time to Pay off Student Loans." Education Data Initiative. December 16. https://educationdata.org/average-time-to-repay-student-loans.

Hanson, Melanie. 2023a. "Average Student Loan Payment." Education Data Initiative. May 30. https://educationdata.org/average-student-loan-payment.

Hanson, Melanie. 2023b. "Student Loan Debt Statistics." Education Data Initiative. July 17. https://educationdata.org/student-loan-debt-statistics.

Hanson, Melanie. 2023c. "College Tuition Inflation Rate." Education Data Initiative. August 13. https://educationdata.org/college-tuition-inflation-rate.

Hess, Abigail Johnson. 2022. "CNBC Survey: 81% of Adults With Student Loans Say They've Had to Delay Key Life Milestones."

CNBC. January 28. www.cnbc.com/2022/01/28/81percent-of-adults-with-student-loans-say-they-delay-key-life-milesto nes.html.

Hinchliffe, Emma. 2023. "Women CEOs Run 10.4% of Fortune 500 Companies. A Quarter of the 52 Leaders Became CEO in the Last Year." Fortune. June 5. https://fortune.com/2023/06/ 05/fortune-500-companies-2023-women-10-percent/.

Jacobson, Rae. 2023. "College Students and Eating Disorders." Child Mind Institute. February 8. https://childmind.org/arti cle/eating-disorders-and-college/.

Johns Hopkins Medicine. 2020. "Genital Herpes." www.hopk insmedicine.org/health/conditions-and-diseases/herpes-hsv1- and-hsv2/genital-herpes.

Kerr, Emma, and Wood, Sarah. 2022. "See How Average Student Loan Debt Has Changed." U.S. News & World Report. September 13. www.usnews.com/education/best-colleges/pay ing-for-college/articles/see-how-student-loan-borrowing-has- changed.

"Know Your IX: What to Know About the Title IX Rule." n.d. Knowyourix.org. https://knowyourix.org/hands-off-ix/basics/.

Kochhar, Rakesh. 2023. "The Enduring Grip of the Gender Pay Gap." Pew Research Center's Social & Demographic Trends Project. March 1. www.pewresearch.org/social-trends/2023/ 03/01/the-enduring-grip-of-the-gender-pay-gap/https://www. pewresearch.org/social-trends/2023/03/01/the-enduring-grip- of-the-gender-pay-gap/.

Krivkovich, Alexis, Wei Wei Liu, Hilary Nguyen, Ishanaa Rambachan, Nicole Robinson, Monne Williams, and Lareina Yee. 2022. "Women in the Workplace 2022." McKinsey & Company. www.mckinsey.com/featured-insights/diversity- and-inclusion/women-in-the-workplace.

Leu, Katherine. 2017. "Beginning College Students Who Change Their Majors Within 3 Years of Enrollment." Data Point.

National Center for Education Statistics. December. https://nces.ed.gov/pubs2018/2018434/index.asp#.

Love Is Respect. 2020. "Types of Abuse." Love Is Respect. www.loveisrespect.org/resources/types-of-abuse/.

Morgenroth, Thekla, Michelle K. Ryan, and Cordelia Fine. 2022. "The Gendered Consequences of Risk-Taking at Work: Are Women Averse to Risk or to Poor Consequences?" *Psychology of Women Quarterly* 46(3). https://doi.org/10.1177/0361684322 1084048.

National Eating Disorder Association. 2017. "Substance Use and Eating Disorders." National Eating Disorders Association. October 5. www.nationaleatingdisorders.org/substance-use-and-eating-disorders.

National Institute of Mental Health. 2023. "Depression." National Institute of Mental Health. April. www.nimh.nih.gov/health/topics/depression.

National Institute on Alcohol Abuse and Alcoholism. n.d. "Alcohol Calorie Calculator—Rethinking Drinking." Rethinking Drinking. National Institutes of Health. http://rethinkingdrinking.niaaa.nih.gov/toolsresources/caloriecalculator.asp.

Nawaz, Amna, and Diane Lincoln Estes. 2022. "People of Color With Eating Disorders Face Cultural, Medical Stigmas." PBS NewsHour. March 28. www.pbs.org/newshour/show/people-of-color-with-eating-disorders-face-cultural-medical-stigmas.

Neal, Stephanie, Rosey Rhyne, Jazmine Boatman, Bruce Watt, and Mindy Yeh. 2023. "Global Leadership Forecast 2023." *DDI World*. www.ddiworld.com/global-leadership-forecast-2023.w

Nova, Annie. 2023. "$6 Billion in College Scholarships Are Awarded Each Year. Here's What You Need to Know about Applying." CNBC. April 4. www.cnbc.com/2023/04/04/everything-students-need-to-know-about-college-scholarships.html.

NVRDC. 2020. "#DVAM2020: Domestic & Dating Violence on College and University Campuses." Network for Victim Recovery of DC. October 30. www.nvrdc.org/blog/2020/10/30/dvam2020-domestic-amp-dating-violence-on-college-and-university-campuses#_ftn1.

O'Connell-Domenech, Alejandra. 2023. "Why Is Gen Z Drinking Less?" The Hill. April 6. https://thehill.com/changing-america/well-being/3936579-why-is-gen-z-drinking-less/.

Parker, Kim, and Cary Funk. 2017. "Gender Discrimination Comes in Many Forms for Today's Working Women." Pew Research Center. December 14. www.pewresearch.org/short-reads/2017/12/14/gender-discrimination-comes-in-many-forms-for-todays-working-women/.

Planned Parenthood. n.d. "STDs and STIs." Planned Parenthood Mar Monte. www.plannedparenthood.org/planned-parenthood-mar-monte/campaigns/stds-stis.

Rape, Abuse and Incest National Network. (n.d.a). "Victims of Sexual Violence: Statistics." www.rainn.org/statistics/victims-sexual-violence.

Rape, Abuse and Incest National Network. (n.d.b). "The Criminal Justice System: Statistics." www.rainn.org/get-information/statistics/reporting-rates.

Rape, Abuse and Incest National Network. (n.d.c). "Sexual Assault." www.rainn.org/articles/sexual-assault.

Rape, Abuse and Incest National Network. (n.d.d). "Perpetrators of Sexual Violence: Statistics." www.rainn.org/statistics/perpetrators-sexual-violence.

Rutgers Center for American Women and Politics. 2023. "Women in Elective Office 2023." Rutgers University. https://cawp.rutgers.edu/facts/current-numbers/women-elective-office-2023.

Schaeffer, Katherine. 2022. "10 Facts about Today's College Graduates." Pew Research Center. April 12. www.pewresearch.org/short-reads/2022/04/12/10-facts-about-todays-college-graduate.

Skinner, Martie L., Allison N. Kristman-Valente, and Todd I. Herrenkohl. 2015. "Adult Binge Drinking: Childhood Sexual Abuse, Gender and the Role of Adolescent Alcohol-Related Experiences." *Alcohol and Alcoholism* 51(2): 136–141. https://doi.org/10.1093/alcalc/agv093.

South, Scott J., and Lei Lei. 2021. "Why Are Fewer Young Adults Having Casual Sex?" *Socius: Sociological Research for a Dynamic World*, March. https://doi.org/10.1177/2378023121996854.

Stalking Prevention, Awareness, and Resource Center. n.d. "Stalking among College Students: Fact Sheet." https://www.stalkingawareness.org/wp-content/uploads/2021/09/Campus-Stalking-Fact-Sheet.pdf.

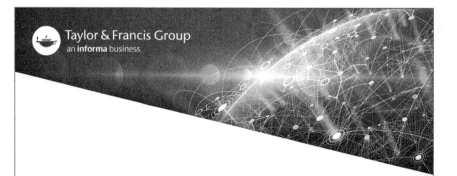

Printed in the United States
by Baker & Taylor Publisher Services